Boatnuts Loose in the Caribbean

Boatnut

Norma and I have been called Boatnuts more than once in our lifetime and when the Word program kept inserting a red line under it every time it was typed, we started wondering just what this term meant. First I checked the dictionary and found no such word. There was a boatman, boatswain, and boathouse; but try as we would, we just couldn't find Boatnut. Next, I checked the Internet. There were plenty of Boatnuts listed and all seemed to be the name of a nautical business. Ah, that's it; it is being used to describe someone who has gone overboard with their enthusiasm for boats.

Grabbing a bottle of Captain Morgan Rum, I sat cross-legged on the floor; poured a glass and prepared the following top ten list to help determine if you too are in danger of being a Boatnut:

1. If your home is decorated with ships' wheels, ship models, boat pictures, mermaids, and lighthouses…

    You might be a Boatnut

2. If your best dress shoes say Sperry on them…

    You might be a Boatnut

3. If your Christmas tree is decorated with nautical ornaments and has a functional lighthouse on top instead of a star…

    You might be a Boatnut

4. If all the jewelry you own consists of little boats, anchors, and ships' wheels…

    You might be a Boatnut

5. If most of your shirts or blouses have nautical themes printed on them…

   You might be a Boatnut

6. If you are an active member of a yacht club, The Seven Seas Cruising Association, The United States Power Squadron or the United States Coast Guard Auxiliary…

   You might be a Boatnut

7. If you know your Boat US membership number by heart…

   You might be a Boatnut

8. If you have a brass clock on any wall that looks like it is built inside a porthole…

   You might be a Boatnut

9. If you have an anchor, sailboat, or mermaid tattooed on any part of your body…

   You might be a Boatnut

10. And finally, if your primary residence has a bow and a stern and floats…

    You are definitely a Boatnut

Preface

Ten, nine, eight, seven, the fire works are already filling the sky across Boca Ciega Bay, flooding it in bright colors. The still night air cannot conceal the thundering booms only associated with larger displays and a strange excitement prevails. Six, five, four, a cooler is descending from a metal yardarm at the famous Boca Ciega Yacht Club in Gulfport, Florida. Three, two, one—the cooler hits the ground and immediately volunteers are distributing its wonderful contents (ice cold champagne) to the screaming, joyful members and guest.

Norma, my bride of nearly 40 years and I took time out from singing for a kiss, and then raised our glasses in celebration of the New Year (2010). This marks the beginning of a new chapter in our lives.

Our Island Packet 44 sailboat, *Happy Ours*, rests quietly in her slip in St Pete Municipal Marina. This will be the first time we have not returned to her on New Years Eve in 8 years, and both of us are quietly saddened.

Last year, we celebrated in Mario's Marina in Guatemala, watching a sizzling fireworks display being launched from a barge in the Rio Dulce River. The year previous, we joined hands with fellow sailors and local Panamanians as we circled the Manaka and revelled as a blazing fire consumed him and symbolically, any unhappiness that had troubled us throughout the year. Previously, there had been great parties in many interesting places, the memories of which are slowly fading away as surely as the sea has swallowed our wake.

Our new home is a condo in Gulfport, Florida and *Happy Ours* is up for sale. The veil of reality is slowly closing on our fantasy life in the Caribbean. Our plans for the future are as unsettled as a cruising sailors plans for his next destination; however, the concept of piloting a barge through Europe's extensive canal system excites both of us.

We must admit, after attending race week in Georgetown, the Carnival in Trinidad, cruising the beautiful windward and leeward islands, partying in Margarita, climbing Angel Falls in Venezuela, and exploring a good part of Central and South America, we both are addicted to adventure as surely as a drug addict must be hooked on what ever is his pleasure.

The question arises "How did a couple from Missouri, so far from the ocean, wind up spending eight years on a sailboat in the Caribbean?" We don't really know for sure, some things just happen and others can be helped along with determination, preparation and a wee bit of luck. Maybe it best serves us to start at the beginning and see how our story unfolds.

To Norma,

My Wife, First Mate

And

Life Long Friend

Contents

Chapter 1	Passion	1
Chapter 2	The Trip to the Bahamas	7
Chapter 3	On to the Virgin Islands	11
Chapter 4	Preparations	17
Chapter 5	Crewing on Wind Dancer	23
Chapter 6	Preparing Our Escape	27
Chapter 7	The Breakdown Cruise	33
Chapter 8	Back to the Bahamas	47
Chapter 9	A Dash to get Below 12.5	55
Chapter 10	Trinidad	63
Chapter 11	On to Venezuela	73
Chapter 12	Inland Travel from Venezuela	85
Chapter 13	Life After Venezuela	101
Chapter 14	Panama	115
Chapter 15	The Western Caribbean	135
Chapter 16	Guatemala	143
Chapter 17	You'd Better Belize It!	157
Chapter 18	A Strange Welcome to Mexico	165
Chapter 19	Back to the USA	177
Chapter 20	Just for Cruisers and the Curious	183

Chapter 1

Passion

Sailing has always been my passion. No one in our family had ever owned or even been on a sailboat. Looking back, I think my interest might have been sparked when, at the age of five, Aunt Frances gave me a picture of a small boat cruising along under its single sail. The picture is mounted on a piece of wood and the whole thing sealed in some kind of protective finish.

Soon afterwards, I built a small wooden model of the boat in my picture and amazed the family who proudly displayed it for many years in Grandma's whatnot cabinet. Little did they or I understand the depth of my enthusiasm for sailboats.

I can remember lying in my bunk bed at night trying to project myself in to that little sailboat, only imagining how it must feel to move thru the waves while silently being driven by the wind.

How free and independent I would feel before falling asleep. The Ocean was a long way from Independence, Missouri and the whole thing became sort of a relaxation ritual that has served me well most of my life.

There was a small lake in Jackson County not far from where we lived. Having earned the all-important driver's license at age sixteen, I would often drive to a favorite spot overlooking Lake Jacomo, and watch the sailboats ghost along in light breezes.

My father purchased an aluminum fourteen-foot fishing boat, which he kept at the lake. It had only a ten-hp motor—the maximum allowed on this type of vessel. Time spent fishing with Dad was enjoyable and it gave me a chance for a closer look at the sailboats and their crews. As sailors seem all over the world, they scarcely gave notice to a young man in a powerboat unless they felt obligated to yell out that they had right of way; something I could use when I would be at the helm of my own sailboat.

I graduated from Van Horn High School in Independence, Missouri in 1963 and immediately disappointed my family by not showing up for the first day at Kansas City Junior College in which I had been enrolled. It was supposed to be cut and dried— graduated in the upper 20% of my class!

I had a job as a bill collector at National Bellas Hess, an Austin Healey Sprite convertible, and a green eyed girlfriend. Who could want more? At my father's insistence, I could either go to trade school, join the military, or find another place to stay.

Very shortly, I enrolled at the Electronics Institute in Kansas City—a move I never regretted, not knowing at the time how important electronic navigation and communications would later be.

One memorable day, I stopped by a gas station belonging to Herb Deets in Englewood. He was always friendly and in conversation, as if he knew about my deepest desire, mentioned his wife Penny had a small sailboat she wanted to sell. I wound up purchasing her fourteen-foot Penguin for $350 including the trailer. It was wood with wooden spars and needed some work. The sails were marked: Ratsey and Lapthorn—1954 and were still in good shape. Varnish was blistering and pealing from the mahogany interior and the hull was in desperate need of a new coat of paint, but to me she was beautiful! Equipped with a centerboard, it could go very shallow with no problem—now I could sail!

Bribing a close friend named Tom Feeny with a case of Coors beer, we headed to lake Jacomo to fulfill a dream. It wasn't difficult to rig the little boat; we had the mast stepped and secure in short order. The launch went well. A long line allowed me to pull her over to the dock after launching, while Tom parked his truck.

Putting the sail up for the first time was an adrenalin rush for both of us; we were cutting thru the water in the ten-knot winds before getting our first beer open. Several beers later, we had mastered every point of sail and were really having fun. We watched how other boats were setting their sails and learned from them.

Of course, on the water, alcohol dulls the brain more rapidly and things can go wrong in a hurry!

"Bob," Tom called out. "I've gotta go drain the ol' lizard. Sail over to the shore and let me off. I'll go behind that clump of trees, and then you can come back and pick me up."

Sounded like a plan—Tom stood on the gunnel, hanging on to the front stay, yelling "hurry."

It happened so quickly we just couldn't believe it. We had forgotten to bring up the centerboard, which promptly struck a submerged rock. Our little boat spun around and violently tossed my friend Tom overboard on to the rocks that lined the lakeshore. Tom lay there for a moment moaning and groaning and, although we never talked about it, I suspect he no longer needed to find a tree.

The aluminum centerboard was bent and we could no longer raise it. Our only option was to wade in and carry the little boat on to the bank, drop the rigging, turn the boat over, and use one of the rocks to beat the centerboard straight. This operation consumed most the remaining time allotted for sailing, as we had no running lights. With the centerboard being reasonably straight, we promptly re-rigged and headed for the dock; all the while laughing and enjoying a great, magical sail into the sunset.

This little sailboat provided several years of fun and each time out, I learned more about sailing. I found my fellow sailors to be friendlier, now that I was one of them, and they would share lots of information about boat handling.

Sunday was a big day on Lake Jacomo for racing: Lightings, Sweet 16's, Hobie cats, Sunfish, and small cruisers up to 26 feet in length, all participated in races sponsored by the Jacomo Cruiser Club. In addition to the sailboats, there were paddleboats, small fishing boats, canoes, and pontoon boats all vying for their small piece of that teeny eleven hundred-acre lake. Just being out on the water without getting involved in a collision required a person's full attention, and a good measure of luck.

It was in this small boat, on this little lake, that I took Norma (my wife to be) for her first sail. It was early in the season and the wooden planks hadn't swelled sufficiently to prevent water from leaking in. Norma, not knowing what to expect, wore a cute little outfit instead of a bathing suit—a mistake we still laugh about.

A good-looking woman who laughed about getting soaked and truly enjoyed sailing certainly intrigued me—we soon married and have been laughing and sailing together for over 40 years.

We saved up our money and enjoyed our honeymoon aboard the *Song of Norway*; at that time one of the newest, most luxurious, cruise ships in the ocean. We enjoyed everything about our cruise in the Caribbean; however, I must admit, we both would have traded places with the cruising people on their own private yachts, with whom we shared the anchorages.

We purchased several sailboats over the following years; fixed them up, sailed and then resold them. Each time we made a small profit. We gained knowledge about the different types of rigs and started forming opinions about our likes and dislikes. The boats became larger and more comfortable with cabins, porta-potties, small galleys, and sleeping quarters.

Our daughter Colleen had become a competent sailor. She was blond, tan, slim, trim, and agile which made her sought after as crew on some of the faster race boats. We joined the Jacomo Cruiser club and enjoyed the many fun activities that go along with boating; however, Norma and I never participated in organized racing. Cruising and relaxing was more our style. There was plenty of unorganized racing; however, and this provided us ample opportunity to hone our sailing skills.

Both the launch ramp and dock at Jacomo provided a stage for some of the most amusing entertainment imaginable. Thank goodness when it was my time to perform, none of my fellow cruisers were there to witness.

We had purchased an eight-cylinder Ford Maverick in 1976. It had sufficient power to pull our eighteen-foot boat and we had installed a trailer hitch for that purpose. When Colleen and I wanted to go sailing during the week, Norma would leave the new little Maverick home and take our other car to work.

My days off were during the week, so the two of us were quite proficient at launching our boat. I would untie it from the trailer at the top of the ramp, raise the centerboard, and tie a long line to the bow fitting. Colleen would take the bowline and stand on the dock. I would back down quickly, hit the brake and our boat would slide effortlessly off the trailer into the water and Colleen would then pull it over to the dock and secure it while I parked the car.

This procedure served us well and we didn't need to back mom's new car as far into the lake. Doing it the slow, boring way of backing in far enough for the boat to float off on its own meant backing the car further into the water.

We were quite proud of having figured this all out on our own until, in my haste to sail, I forgot to raise the centerboard. It rested in a cradle on the trailer until we were in the water, then it pivoted deeper for stability when we released a cable. Unfortunately, without the cable being locked in the raise position, the centerboard dropped down immediately when the boat started sliding off. It slammed into the back cross member of the trailer and the momentum pulled the trailer with Norma's new little car still attached into the lake. It all stopped sliding when the boat floated off and the trailer wheels slipped off the end of the concrete ramp into the muck.

The faithful car kept running even though water was up to the edge of the driver's seat. I tried in vain to drive out but the trailer being over the edge of the concrete, held it all in place as surely as if we had been anchored.

I left the car running, opened the door and climbed out to assess the situation. Colleen was laughing in a strange sort of shocked amusement. She described it as "And here was dad with a wet cigarette flopping up and down in his mouth due to all the cussing. All the while his tennis shoes were going squish, squish, and squish as he stomped up the ramp."

Luckily, there was a parks department crew working nearby and they had a large truck and some chain. One of them, a big ol' guy was laughing so hard he was literally lying on his belly beating the ground with his fist! I really didn't think it was that funny, but he was huge and he did have the truck. When he finally quit laughing, he and his crew dragged the car and trailer out and helped us load up the boat.

After dropping the boat off at the house, we headed for the car wash, stripped out the back seat and all of the carpet, and quickly washed things down. I swore Colleen to secrecy; bought a round of Big Macks, and went home. We hung the carpet on our backyard fence to dry in the sun, and used hairdryers on the interior. By the time Norma arrived home, all looked normal—So we thought!

Summer passed and with the Missouri fall came cold weather. Norma started complaining that the windows would fog up on the inside and the defroster just wouldn't clear it. She also mentioned smelling a strange foul odor when she ran the heater. As winter brought freezing weather, the fog problem was worse than ever—frost was forming on the inside of the windows instead of on the outside where it belonged. The transmission started acting up also. (A little lake water must have gotten in.)

"Darn Ford, it must be a lemon; let's get rid of it." We traded it in and although conscience might have bothered a lesser man, I was just glad to see it go.

Colleen had kept quiet for months until one day Norma started talking about how bad that car had smelled. She said, "It even smelled a little like fish," and also speculated that maybe I had been passing gas in her car. That did it!

Colleen couldn't contain it any longer and asked, "Can I tell her dad?" I agreed it had gone on long enough. Colleen's version contained some embellishment but sounded so funny we couldn't help but laugh. Even great captains can have a bad day!

Chapter 2

The Trip to the Bahamas

Several members of the Jacomo sailing club shared their excitement of chartering sailboats in the Bahamas and the Virgin Islands. We listened intently about their adventures and we decided it was time to try it ourselves. It was suggested that we start with the Bahamas first as it was easier sailing in contrast to the more open and exposed Virgin Islands.

    Jim and Helen McMullen, two of the members that had been to the Bahamas several times, were going again with their daughter Jana, son Jeff, and his wife Kim. Jim was a criminal defense attorney who during the week wore a 3-piece suit and was well known in the courts of Kansas City for his success in representing clients. Evenings and weekends would find him in old worn t-shirts and shorts raising cain on his boat. Helen was an equal partner; the judge that presided over their 40th anniversary party dubbed her "Saint Helen," for putting up with all of Jimmy's bull.

    They insisted we get a crew and come with them on our own charter boat. We chose our neighbors, Russlyn and Larry Large to accompany us on our first sail in salt water. They had no sailing experience except being with us on Jacomo. Russlyn didn't want to handle the boat and agreed to be only the cook. Larry, on the other hand was game for anything.

    The first morning aboard, while we were waiting for someone to come and go thru the equipment list and checkout procedure, we decided to go for a swim in the beautiful clear waters. We all dived in and were swimming around when Larry started screaming as he started swimming like crazy towards the dink. Terrified, we all headed for the ladder on the boat and quickly exited the water. When we were safe, we asked Larry what he saw. "Turds, turds all over the place" he yelled from the dink. Looking around I could see what he was talking about. We learned later not to swim in a crowded anchorage in the morning until the tide carries out the mess.

The chart supplied by the charter company was merely a black and white sketch chart glued on to a piece of wood and was sadly lacking in detail. We had no idea of the draft of our CSY 33 and were told just to stay where the water was less white, and to stay out of the dark brown stuff. I had no knowledge of chart kits or cruising guides and we were sadly unprepared for things to come.

We followed our friend Jim around for several days, running aground only once, before we were ready to take the lead. Jim knew the area well and could easily direct us using the VHF.

As luck would have it, on the third day out, the beautiful blue sky suddenly gave way to a horizon full of the darkness that warns of an impending storm. The winds became so strong we were wearing dive masks and snorkels at the helm to enable us to see and breathe.

We were being beat senseless by the wind driven rain and the putrid greenish, sand filled breaking waves that occur in shallow water. The surrounding black clouds were filled with the high voltage discharges of terrifying lightening strikes and our 50ft tall mast seemed to invite disaster as it waved in the sky.

As cook, Russlyn bravely went below and rolled up sandwiches by squeezing them between her fingers. She timed the waves, and passed us food by opening a hatch and handing the sandwiches out one at a time. We were famished—It was nearly dark and we hadn't eaten since breakfast. We opened a round of cold beers to drink but this turned into a disaster as salt water quickly contaminated the contents of the cans.

There was not enough detail on the chart to help us decide where to go for shelter and it was on that day I vowed to take a boating course and learn more about navigation.

Emergency aerial flares dotted the sky all around us, and radio messages from fellow mariners screaming out for help dominated Channel sixteen on the radio. I tried to call Jim several times but never got an answer. Reluctantly, I swallowed my pride and keyed the microphone on the VHF radio:

" Abaco Bahamas Charters, Abaco Bahamas Charters,

This the sailing vessel Alcazar."(By now Norma had re-named it Alcatraz)

"This is the Abaco Bahamas Charters, What can we do for you Mon?"

"We are under sail, it is getting dark, the motor overheats running against the wind and we believe we're actually going backwards and sideways under reefed main and jib. Will our draft allow us to fall off, go behind the little islands and anchor at Man O War?"

" Mon, we see you now, just fall off and sail straight towards Man O War and anchor with d' other boats you see over there".

"How the Hell can you see us all the way from Hope Town?" I blurted out in frustration.

"Mon, we are here assisting your friend Jimmy who has lost his main sail and had a nasty fall. Enough talk, get your buts over to the anchorage, drop both anchors at a 45 degree Angel to each other, and let out all of the chain."

Turned out Jimmy was ok, they guided him in and anchored him next to us. Even at anchor the boats were pitching and rolling, all the while tugging violently against the anchor chains. There was not much sleeping that night as we could hear the waves breaking violently on the reef behind us. The storm passed the next day and all was well, except they charged Jimmy an extra thousand dollars to replace the mainsail. It took a day for the waves to calm down so we spent the time exploring Man of War.

In the following days, the beautiful Bahama Islands lived up to their reputation; crystal clear water, bright sunshine, smooth sailing, friendly people, and a delightful rum concoction call a "Goombay Smasher." We swam, ate seafood, drank, partied, and sailed.

The last night there, we turned in Alcazar and took rooms at Hopetown in order to stage for our flight home in the morning.

There were only two rooms available—one in the main lodge and the other, a quaint cottage on the beach. Of course, we all wanted the cottage so we flipped a coin. Russlyn and Larry won, so Norma and I headed to the lodge to store our luggage. Our room was clean and nice but Norma was still unhappy about not winning the coin toss.

After we settled in, it was time to check with our friends and take a swim. We broke out some cold beers and some left over snacks and headed down to their cottage. While we were chatting, movement caught my attention out of the corner of my eye. To our horror, some strange looking bugs had gathered up a chip someone had dropped and were carrying it off across the floor. The place was infested with bugs and Norma no longer complained about our nice clean room.

Our time went buy much too quickly and we found ourselves on a water taxi heading for the airport, wishing we could have stayed longer. Russlyn and Larry were still friends so we figured the trip was a success.

Jim and his crew left the day before us and when we gathered at his house a couple of weeks later; we all enjoyed re-living the experience.

Chapter 3

On to the Virgin Islands

Returning to our Chrysler 26, we found the boat to be fine; however, the lake had shrunk considerably. The following Sunday, after a near collision with one of the race boats, we had had enough. It was time to find larger water.

Ted and Joyce Rice (of TJ Cinnamon fame) had previously left Jacomo to sail on Truman Lake and encouraged us to bring our boat to Truman State Park Marina and join them. We did, and were soon followed by Don Birkness, Dave Beaulieu, our old friends from the Bahamas trip—Jim and Helen McMullen, Fred and Mary Kay Kerns (some long time sailing friends), and their son Greg.

This lake was formed when the Corp of Engineers built Truman Dam near Warsaw, Missouri and was known as one of the best fishing lakes in the area; however, the water was as muddy as the Missouri River and it was full of trees in its shallows.

We shared the marina with houseboats, pontoon boats and dozens of fishing boats. The lake was not crowded and boasted a beautiful, unspoiled shoreline. Although we missed all of the social activities at Jacomo, there was plenty of unorganized fun to be had. We swapped boat rides with some house boaters (Bob and Sandy Orlinger and John and Fran DeCloud) and had so much fun that our old friends Jimmy and Helen McMullen and Fred and Mary Kay Kerns sold their sailboats and opted for the more spacious accommodations of a houseboat.

We raised our fishing skills to new levels, as there were plenty of fish to go around. John and Jimmy showed me the easiest method for catching and cleaning the different types of fish—another skill we would find useful while cruising. Some of the fishing fun stays with me today—I remember catching a 6-pound bass near sunset and I can still close my eyes and picture him dancing on his tail across the water, his silhouette back dropped by the beautiful golden sunset that surrounded us. I must admit that he was delicious. Our friend Jim yelled in pain when he found out that we ate the fish instead of returning it to be caught another time. Catch and release? It has always been catch and eat for us!

Norma and I soon purchased a Newport 30 sailboat—no houseboat for us! It was sloop rigged and equipped with an inboard diesel engine—just like the boats we had chartered. We named her *Fantasea* and would stay on her a week at a time, enjoying the spacious cabin, air-conditioning, and all her amenities. We read *Cruising World Magazine* faithfully and practiced the art of living aboard as much as we could.

John and Fran's houseboat was just down the dock from us and we would often meet for cocktails at sunset with others on the dock. John had flown Corsairs off the deck of a carrier in WW2 and had lots of good stories to tell. He always seemed to know how to do things such as belaying cleats, tying knots, etc.

When I asked where he had learned so much about boating, he told me it was from courses he had taken in the United States Power Squadron. He went on to explain it was for both sail and power enthusiast, and invited us to attend a meeting.

Norma and I both signed up and completed the basic boating course—a prerequisite for becoming members. Once members, advanced courses such as piloting, navigation, weather, and engine maintenance were made available to us. We both enrolled in what ever was being taught, but unfortunately, Norma couldn't attend all of the courses because of her job as a tax preparer.

Often John and I would monitor channel sixteen on the VHF and in the absence of the local water patrol, would go to the rescue of those needing help on Truman Lake. Several times we climbed into John's little runabout, fired up the trusty 65 hp outboard motor and head out in search of whoever was calling for help. Proper towing techniques were part of our teachings and it was fun to look as professional as possible.

The skills we learned from the Power Squadron gave us confidence and certainly made us safer, more reliable members of the boating community. We became involved with the organization and I wound up being Commander of the Kansas City Power Squadron, on to Commander of District 30 and finally received an appointment to the National Safety Committee. Norma, following her passion for numbers, served on various committees and was assistant treasurer for District 30.

All of this new knowledge begged to be put to use! Three couples from Truman Lake (Dr. Don and Dr. Carolyn Birkness, Dr. Dave and Florence Beaulieu, Norma and myself) decided to take the next step in chartering and headed for the Virgin Islands.

We chartered an Oday 39 sloop and left out of Charlotte Amalya for a fascinating ten-day cruise of both the British and American Virgin Islands. As with nearly every cruise, there was an element of danger and excitement. The weather was unsettled, leaving plenty of wind and waves to keep us entertained.

When first boarding *Symphony*, we celebrated with a round of drinks and hoisted our old Lake Jacomo yacht club burgee for the entire world to see. It hadn't even unfurled when a young man with a super dark tan and an athletic build stopped in his tracks on the dock and asked with a smirk "What is that?" "Where are you from?"

"That is our yacht club burgee," Donald offered.

"We're down here from the Kansas City area," I replied.

"I didn't know they had yacht clubs and sailors in Kansas City," he sneered.

"Give us a couple of days to get acquainted with this boat and look us up. We'll show you what KC sailors can do!"

He laughed out loud and walked confidently down the dock. It turned out he was a sailing instructor working out of our marina. We never figured out what his problem was, but we detected an instant dislike on his part for all of us.

Rounding Red Buoy #2, into the open channel, Norma and Carolyn, who were setting on the bow, disappeared under the waves twice before scurrying back to the safety of the cockpit. At least two hours of beauty parlor hairdos were destroyed in a heartbeat! All the while, Florence, with a still perfect hairdo, was loosing her breakfast overboard. The bananas that had been on her cereal were mostly recognizable as they washed around on deck and I found myself looking at the horizon and deep breathing to keep from joining her at the rail. We were sailing!

Having learned from our previous charter in the Bahamas, this time we showed up with our own charts, and cruising guide. All on board were competent lake sailors and confidence soon replaced fear. The six to eight foot waves were the biggest we had ever seen and the trade winds were howling at twenty to twenty-five knots. We could see why it is recommended to charter in the Bahamas a couple of times before heading to the Virgin Islands.

These islands are further apart and sailing is more exposed to the fetch of the open ocean. Some of the island chain is considered part of the United States and the rest is under British rule. The water is deeper than in the Bahamas and has a more intense darker blue color in the deep, graduating to various shades of beautiful emerald green as your eye wanders towards the gorgeous white sand beaches.

The Oday 39 was new and in good shape—a big contrast to our charter boat in the Bahamas. We provisioned the boat ourselves; doing is the best way to learn. Once under weigh getting to a destination before nightfall, as required by our charter agreement, was no problem in the strong trade winds with this lively yacht.

We did it all! Explored the Baths, snorkeled on the wreck of the Rhone, dinked into partially flooded caves, sailed in to a British harbor and cleared customs for the first time, and visited the famous Bitter End Yacht Club.

Each morning, we held a brief meeting to decide our day's agenda, and found planning was easy with the use of our cruising guide. The chart kit contained up to date information, and Power Squadron knowledge helped us safely navigate. Nearly every destination had an interesting restaurant and bar catering to cruisers—life was good!

Our six-person crew was all friends and even in the confines of living on the sailboat together, got along very well. One problem occurred, however, because of cigarette smoking. David was the only smoker in the crowd and agreed to limit his smoking to only in the cockpit. This worked out fine except in the strong wind, ashes would fly everywhere from the miniature blowtorch.

Don was on watch and I was relaxing when all of a sudden, Don grabbed his face in pain and let out a loud groan. His over six foot tall stature staggering around blindly in the stern of the boat, while carrying on like a mad man, reminded me of the Giant Cyclops in the movie when he got his eye put out.

Hot ashes from David's cigarette found their way into Don's eyes and he was clearly in pain and angry. David of course was sorry and agreed to be more careful; however, tension existed between the two of them over this event.

In the afternoon, on the fifth day of our charter, the wind and seas had picked up, and we had labored to put a reef in the main in order to shorten sail. We could see a large sailing yacht heeled over under full sail creeping up on our stern. It quickly overhauled us, luffed us up by sailing to our windward (stealing our wind) and continued on ahead. We all recognized the tan; sneering face of the helmsman and the adrenalin started pumping!

Without a spoken word, we shook the reef out of the mainsail, and the clanking of the winch was the only sound to be heard over the roar of the sea. He headed out into the open ocean with us in hot pursuit and although we had shortened the distance between us, we still lacked the ability to point higher into the wind and pass him.

Conditions were deteriorating rapidly and the sky was now filled with ominous dark clouds. All of a sudden, a large rogue wave hit our tormentor, taking him violently to its crest, and then slamming him quickly down its other side. His dink remained airborne, however, and spun around in the sky as if it were an out of control kite. The outboard motor flew off and was lost in the deep blue ocean as were all the dink's contents.

Dave Beaulieu barely had time to gasp, "look at that," before the wave was upon us. Up and over we went and found ourselves surfing at top speed down a seemingly endless slope of water. There wasn't enough time to realize what was happening and we slammed bow first into the foaming ocean. *Symphony* shuddered and we blinked in disbelief as the entire bow disappeared as far up as the mast, and then bobbed up to meet the next wave. The motion was so violent that some cabinet doors were ripped off of their hinges down below and the contents were rolling around on the cabin sole. Dave had left the front hatch open and his bunk was soaked.

We were just a few boat lengths behind and we re-adjusted our course when the boat ahead tacked off to port, the skipper nodded, then waved and sailed off into the gloom. His sneer was gone.

We fell off to starboard and headed for the protection provided by the lee of some of the islands, never to cross paths with this character again. We still had a dink and motor, and enjoyed the rest of the charter with the pride of surviving the ordeal nearly untouched.

We remounted the door hinges by sticking toothpicks in the screw holes and lashed the front cushions to the foredeck to dry in the sun. Nothing else had been damaged, not even our egos.

The Virgin Islands are beautiful and we all truly enjoyed our charter. We made it as far as the Bitter End Yacht Club, leaving there with plenty of Pussers Rum, an armload of souvenirs from their company store and lots of new stories to share.

Chapter 4

Preparations

We sailed for several happy years on Truman Lake, enjoying our friends, both old and new. As time passed, we found ourselves wanting cleaner water and a larger group of sail boaters with which to interface. By then, more than half of the crowd that moved to Truman Lake with us had either purchased house boats or had moved on to other lakes.

Looking around, we decided to relocate *Fantasea* to Lake Stockton in Missouri, a longer drive but clean water and a very large sailing community made it an attractive choice. As a bonus, on windless, hot weekends, it was only an hour drive to Springfield and not far from Branson. We both love country music and Branson is a great place to take in live shows of some of the biggest names in country music.

We joined Lake Stockton Yacht Club and took part in the many activities it offered. Ron and Jennifer Plymate had purchased Orleans Trail, a rundown marina and turned it into a very nice, safe place to leave our boat.

It was told that when Ron suffered a heart attack and was lying on the dock waiting for the ambulance to arrive, he asked some one to bring a hammer so he could drive in two nails that were sticking up. I'm not sure this is true but Ron has that kind of personality. We had found a new home!

We all sailed and enjoyed anchoring out in the many beautiful coves, and Ron and Jennifer hosted most of the Yacht Club events in their marina.

The water in Stockton Lake was clear enough that dive shops came down for their open water dives. I became interested in diving and was convinced it would be a necessary skill for ocean cruising. Norma gave me a certificate for dive lessons for the two of us at *Skin and Scuba* in Independence for my fiftieth birthday. We both learned a great deal about diving, swimming, snorkeling, floating, and ourselves.

It turned out that Norma had a big problem with claustrophobia. She tried very hard to fight her fear and had passed all of her pool work as well as the written exams. After having a really difficult night practicing "doff and don," (taking off all of the dive equipment and putting it back on at the bottom of the pool), She had had enough.

Each of us in turn would demonstrate our proficiency, then remain down and watch as our fellow students took their turn. Norma completed this with flying colors but she couldn't stand just being down there with nothing to do but listen to herself breathe. Panic took over and she headed for the surface. One of the dive masters tried to slow her ascent by grabbing her ankle and she just hit a button, inflated her Buoyancy Compensator, and they both rocketed to the top. Rapid assent is a very dangerous move in deep water and even though we were training in a pool, what she did was a real no-no.

We were driving a little red sports car and the top was down that night. On the way home, I stopped at a red light, which placed us directly under a bright streetlight. We had been silent up until this point and I was shocked when I looked her in the face. What I saw was two big bloodshot eyes glaring at me. The shadows from the streetlight gave her a sinister look that reminded me of a demon from the deep. Silence was broken when she growled, "This is another fine freaking mess you have gotten me into!" I knew she had enough.

I was able to pass the open water test and received certification—another step closer to going cruising and Norma knew how to give a buddy check.

We started looking around for other skills that we might require while sailing on the ocean. By then, I had earned an associate degree in electronic engineering technology and had taken a promotion at Kansas City Power and Light. I found myself becoming less and less energetic as my new job required many long hours setting at a desk. I reasoned having strength and agility was as important as navigation skills and began searching for a way to get back into shape.

Having visited several gymnasiums, I decided that their type of exercise would soon become boring and I would not stay with it. My company offered a fitness program that would pay most of the cost, but required many visits a year, making it expensive for me to drop out.

I reasoned that Karate certainly would provide plenty of exercise and skills that might come in handy. Norma, still smarting from the scuba classes wanted no part of it.

I started visiting dojos in search of the right one. I was very disappointed; most of the ones I visited reminded me of the dance class I had attended as a young man at Aunt Louise's studio.

Suddenly, there it was! The Yellow Pages produced an add for a dojo that boasted "This ain't a dance class."(Really) Calling the phone number landed me a free trial lesson at Katzer's Bushidokan in Raytown.

The class started out with stretching exercises, then continued on to knuckle push-ups, leg lifts, and other forms a calisthenics. This was followed by a heavy bag workout, where we practiced kicking and punching an 80-pound bag until it won. Specialized training followed all of this with instructions on the various self-defenses.

One day a week was set aside for light contact kick boxing and it took several months of nosebleeds, black eyes, and bruises before I learned to block and dodge. I remember coming home after a having a really difficult class. I had taken a punch square in the nose and must have resembled W. C. Fields. Crimson blood covered a great deal of my snow-white gi as a testimony to my skill level. My next-door neighbor, Dr. Baker watched intently as I climbed out of my truck. "You are getting too darn old for that my boy," he said as he shook his head and came over to inspect the damage. Luckily nothing was broken.

Having worked out three times a week for over five years certainly improved me physically and the skills I learned from this nontraditional "what ever it takes " type training proved more than useful, as we will see later.

Obtaining a general class ham operator's license was a suggestion listed in a Seven Seas Cruising Association publication. There are radio nets exclusively for sailors having ham licenses that provide valuable cruising information and a chance for forming new friendships.

Free radio e-mail and weather downloads is another important benefit. I hated learning Morse code, however finally, with a head full of ditz and das; I passed the test and became a ham. (Code test are no longer a requirement).

On a recommendation from Skip and Sandra, we joined the Seven Seas Cruising Association and devoured every page of their publications. Members write articles about their experiences in different cruising locations throughout the world. They give advice on where to anchor, what to do, how to clear customs, and some even share waypoints and other sailing instructions.

The SSCA organization hosts great parties and informative events. It was one of our most valuable resources as we traveled through out the Caribbean.

Norma has specialized skills of her own, not only is she an accomplished seamstress, she can cook very well, and organized our small galley to maximize its useful storage capability. In her research, she discovered the importance of having a pressure cooker on board as well as a stackable set of pots and pans. She started purchasing these items and practiced using them on our Lake boat, which had grown into a beautiful Catalina 34 sloop named *Shenanigan*.

It was Norma's turn to name the new boat and She was determined to name it *Happy Days*, a name that just didn't fit. After days of negotiations, we agreed to submit three names each and choose from one of the six. Hearing my choices—*Amazing Disgrace*, *Cirrhosis of the River*, and *Shenanigan*, she was afraid to push this any further and agreed to let me display a wee bit of me Irish heritage.

Perhaps one of Norma's greatest talents arose out of her passion for keeping records. One of our biggest questions was "Can we afford to go cruising, what does it cost?" It was difficult to find up to date information on that subject.

Luckily, we met Pat and Aggie Mora who had just returned to the Kansas City area from spending several years on their sailboat in the Caribbean. Pat, like Norma was an excellent record keeper and gave us a nearly complete list of their expenditures over the past several years afloat. Norma used this list as a guide for making her own. She was able to formulate a useful budget as a guide; something we desperately needed.

Chapter 5

Crewing on Wind Dancer

Friends we made in the Power Squadron, Skip and Sandra Kelly, became very dear to us. We would invite them to come sail on both Truman and Stockton lakes, and the four of us would live aboard in harmony for up to a week at a time. They shared the same passion for cruising on the ocean under sail and eagerly took part in any on the water activities available. They sailed a small boat on Lake Latawana; however, it had neither cabin nor inboard motor.

We often exchanged ideas and dreamed of our escapes to the ocean. They retired ahead of us, purchased a brand new Caliber 38 LRC, (*Wind Dancer*) and invited us to join them on their shakedown cruise in the Gulf of Mexico. How could we refuse!

We sailed out of the Manatee River and headed south towards Key West. Not everything worked perfectly on their new yacht, but overall she was comfortable and sea worthy. We quickly identified the few problems to be referred to the dealer for repair and continued on to our destination.

Sailing into Key West for the first time only fueled our desire to retire and start our own adventure. The bars were full of sailors and their stories. Music, booze, and dancing supplemented the fun and we found there was much more to see and do there than we had imagined.

Skip and I hooked up with a dive shop and enjoyed two days of diving the beautiful keys (my first saltwater diving experience). Other than needing fewer weights because of the difference in buoyancy of not wearing a seven-mill wet suit, and dealing with stronger waves and currents, diving in the crystal clear salt water was an experience I was prepared for. Every minute was filled with seeing beautiful brightly colored fish, coral, and strangely animated seaweed that seemed to possess a life of it's own as it waved eerily in the depths.

Having taken a PADI course on reef ecology, I was able to identify most of what I saw, which added greatly to the fun. Skip, being a more experienced diver, proved to be an excellent and patient dive buddy. I learned from him a shallow breathing technique that allowed the tank air to last longer and a few buoyancy tips to help me keep from damaging the coral.

Sandra could swim and free dive better than most, but had problems with her ears at depth. She and Norma would snorkel and boast about having seen as much as Skip and I did diving in the crystal clear water. I think they were probably right, but not entirely.

We sailed back up to Palmetto from Key West, exploring many beautiful anchorages on the west coast of Florida along the way. Skip and Sandra returned *Wind Dancer* to the dealer for the minor repairs that were needed, then prepared to begin their cruising life. Norma and I went back to work with dreams of our own.

Twice again, we were invited to sail with them—each a priceless adventure. Once we flew to Nassau, and from there explored the Bahamas, then sailed across the Gulf Stream back to the US.

This was our first overnight trip and the magic of being in the ocean at night was breathtaking. Brighter than normal stars twinkled in the heavens above while, at the same time, lightning from a distant storm noiselessly illuminated the northern sky. We saw no other vessels that night and were left alone to ponder the fluorescents of our wake as it disappeared into the dark water behind us.

The last time we sailed with them was from St. Lucia to Union Island. This trip was to shape our destiny. Skip had a small dink and motor. It provided a wet ride for the four of us; however, it was ok for just the two of them. They were traveling with Carl and Mary Lou, some loveable Texans, on *Starlight Dancer* and Rich and Bobbie on *Hideaway*. One afternoon, Rich and Bobbie, who owned a larger dink and motor, invited us to ride back from lunch with them—an arrangement beneficial to all, and we accepted.

On the way back to *Wind Dancer*, Rich asked if we had ever seen inside an Island Packet 44 and invited us aboard their beautiful boat. We jumped at the chance to see it! They were gracious hosts and gave us the five-dollar tour. I silently admired nearly everything about their boat. I could have almost heard Jaws music as they quickly came up behind us the previous day under sail and promptly overhauled the lively *Wind Dancer*. We enjoyed our cruise down to Union Island, exploring the beautiful anchorages along the way, all the while keeping an eye on how well *Hideaway* sailed.

Skip and I celebrated our May birthdays together, giving the eight of us another chance to party while anchored somewhere in the Leeward Islands. Norma and I had been accepted as friends and were treated as fellow cruisers. There was no doubt we would soon be following in their wake.

We had matured as sailors, and were just waiting for the chance to retire and head for the Caribbean. On the flight home, I reluctantly looked at Norma and asked, "What did you think of the Island Packet 44?"

"I loved it, they are a very expensive, well made boat—nicest we have seen. I wish we could afford one." was her surprising reply. We flew back to Kansas City with a common dream of ownership of one of these beautiful boats.

Chapter 6

Preparing Our Escape

The following years flew by as we continued to prepare for retirement. We were both lucky in our careers; the house mortgage was paid off as well as the ones on the cars, truck, and our Catalina 34 sailboat.

We had attended the Annapolis Sailboat Show and met Jennifer with Wagner Stevens Yachts. Over the next several months, Jennifer showed us a variety of boats, in several locations, finally agreeing to watch for an Island Packet 44. The limited production of this model (thirty-nine) made it difficult for us to find one on our own and she faithfully notified us as any of them came available.

We flew to Baltimore to see one, but it wasn't for us. It lacked the necessary cruising equipment and, for the price, displayed none of factory amenities that we so desired. The next trip took us to Ft Lauderdale, Florida, but we were disappointed to learn there was already a contract written on the boat we had come to see.

Jennifer, as we were preparing to leave for home, checked with her office in desperation. She learned an Island Packet 44 had just come on the market and was across the state in Palmetto. We hopped on a plane the next morning, flew to the west coast of Florida, rented a car, and headed for Regatta Point Marina. *Happy Ours* was bouncing gently in her slip, her Island Packet tan gel coat gleaming in the bright sun. She was cutter rigged, and had davits and a dive platform on her stern. Her teak was properly varnished and the stainless sparkled. The burgundy dodger and bimni had seen better days and needed replacing but were well designed.

Below, the cushions were worn and torn but otherwise she was in good shape. The engine was a sixty-two-hp Yanmar with only twelve hundred hours and there was a five-kw Northern Lights diesel generator mounted transversely in the stern. A bow thruster, roller-furling sails (including the main), a water maker, and some power winches topped the equipment list, which was so long it wouldn't fit on one typewritten page.

We eventually made and offer subject to sea trial and survey. The survey didn't go well, there was a page long list of discrepancies; however, she sailed like a dream. The owner agreed to repair all of the problems listed and the deal was done. We returned a few weeks later, re-inspected, then finalized the paper work. When we were handed the keys, we knew they were the keys to the world!

We spent part of November living aboard in the marina, familiarizing ourselves with our new boat and taking bids on canvas work and cushions. Before returning home we took her over to Snead Island for haul out, bottom paint, and storage.

A few months later, at age fifty-six, I completed thirty-one years of service with KCPL, which qualified me for a cash buyout retirement. Norma finished her last season as an Office Manager with HR Block and we were ready to go. We sold our Catalina 34 to a fellow sailor at Stockton, but kept the cooking utensils etc. for the new boat.

We listed our house and hired Angels Auction Service to auction off our belongings—it's nice to have an Angel on your side! These things were now just "stuff" that needed to be disposed of. The cost of storing them would soon exceed the cost of replacement.

Our Daughter Colleen now lived in St Louis and was told to come and get whatever she wanted before the auction. She agreed to store the few plastic tubs of pictures and other things we couldn't bring ourselves to part with and loaded them up with what she wanted to take for herself.

The auction started at seven AM and went to six P.M that evening. It was exhausting. People were asking us questions about all kinds of things. Thank goodness Norma's family showed up to help.

Late in the afternoon, the auction had moved to the back yard where our lawn equipment was on display. Norma and I slipped off into the kitchen and found the last two remaining beers, which now resided in someone else's refrigerator. Popping the tops, we toasted the occasion and leaned against the breakfast bar to enjoy our find.

While we were sipping away, a young couple walked thru our open patio doors and looked around. One said to the other "It's too bad, these people had everything to live for. Wonder what happened to them." We looked at each other in astonishment, clicked our cans together and enjoyed the moment.

The only transportation we had left was our Ford Ranger pick up, loaded full of things to go to the new boat. We called Snead Island Boat works in Florida and asked that they launch *Happy Ours* and have her ready to go when we arrived.

We picked her up, took her back to Regatta Point Marina, secured a slip, and began moving in. It took nearly two full days to shuttle the contents of our truck to the boat with a two-wheel cart provided by the marina.

Norma carefully set up the galley and made a list of things she needed to complete the task. I busied myself storing safety equip.ment and tools. Clothes, towels, and toiletries were put away as we negotiated with each other for the precious available space. The nav station was set up with charts and cruising books we had purchased in anticipation of new destinations, and a Garmin GPS 48 was proudly displayed in its new plastic mount at the helm.

We had invited Allan and Sharon Christensen; fellow cruisers from as far back as Lake Jacomo, to accompany us on our shake down cruise. We chose to sail out of the Manatee River and head North, under the Skyway Bridge, up to St Pete and anchor in the North Basin. There was to be a fireworks display on the water as well as an event hosted by the local restaurants for the sampling of their best recipes.

Every thing went well, we sailed in moderate breezes and eventually found our destination and anchored in the north basin. It was a warm day and we soon dived overboard for a refreshing swim. We were just enjoying the early afternoon swim, minding our own business, when a couple of fellows motored up to us in their dink and suggested we get out of the water because of the large numbers of aggressive bull sharks in the bay.

We thanked them and quickly climbed the boarding ladder back into the safety of the boat. (Ever seen Daffy Duck walk on water in the cartoons?) We were skeptical, having never heard of a bull shark and laughed at each other about having been taken in by a bad joke; however, I went below to check our new fish identification book just in case.

Our eyes widened as I read that there were indeed bull sharks and that they were very aggressive during the then current mating season! We downed some brewskies to celebrate our good fortune of still being in one piece, as we rinsed off the salt water with the cockpit shower and dressed for the evening's fun.

The whole down town area was full of bikers and boaters and the waterfront was sprinkled with tents full of good things to eat and drink. When we dinked back to *Happy Ours* with our bellies full, we were treated to a magnificent fireworks display, which was nearly overhead. What a great first outing.

Sailing back towards our marina, the following night was spent anchored in the Manatee River in front of a little park displaying a white cross as a landmark. Holding was not too good and we nervously took turns checking our position throughout the night. We excitedly relived every detail of our first cruise on *Happy Ours* that evening over cocktails, and started planning our next adventure.

Manually adding waypoints into the GPS one at a time was a time consuming and tedious process, but well worth it. It would beep when it was time to change course and an arrow would show the direction to turn. When the turn was completed, we sat the autopilot on auto and took turns monitoring our progress.

As we were taught in the Power Squadron, we faithfully marked our position on paper charts each hour, as well as when making course changes or taking a fix on nearby landmarks.

At the nav station below was a laptop computer on which was installed the *Capn*, an electronic charting and navigation program.

It displayed our position using the GPS data. Our track was displayed on the electronic chart as well, and was stored away in the computer for future reference.

Allen was blessed with computer skills and this, combined with my electronics background set the stage for improvements in the way *Happy Ours'* cumbersome navigation system worked. Pouring over the manuals, we discovered that the waypoints could be entered in the GPS directly from the *Capn* program in the computer. Furthermore, the same GPS could be set up to drive the autopilot directly. The following day, we went to work re-wiring the nav system and all went as planed; however, neither of us was able to figure out how to insert waypoints into the Garmin GPS using the *Capn* program.

That evening, I received a call that there was a family emergency, so we all piled in our vehicle and headed back for Kansas City. We were there two weeks before returning to Florida.

Hurricane season was upon us and it was a mad dash to provision and get *Happy Ours* and ourselves out of harm's way. Allen and Sharon wanted to sail with us for as long as they could get vacation. It was their desire to gain as much saltwater experience as possible in preparation for their own escape to the cruising life.

Chapter 7

The Breakdown Cruise

We still hadn't figured out how to import waypoints from *Capn* charts into the GPS, and 30 minutes before we were to leave on the rising tide, Allen called Garmin from the marina pay phone for assistance. He came running down the dock with a big ol' grin and climbed aboard. Success! Our entire route was programmed into the GPS in a matter of seconds and off we went! *Happy Ours* motored out of the marina on a rising tide and down the Manatee River with out a hitch. We carefully watched as the little GPS drove the autopilot system. What an improvement!

Our plan was to stop in Venice the first night, stay in a marina, and then work our way down Florida's west coast, but nothing went as planned. Arriving in Venice late in the afternoon, we encountered a cross current so strong it was impossible to get *Happy Ours* into the marina slip, even using the bow thruster. We came close after several attempts only to put the first dent in the bow pulpit as the current smacked us into a piling.

Giving up, we headed up the inlet into the ICW where we promptly ran aground. Lowering the dink, we took an anchor out and set it in deeper water and tried to kedge off by pulling on the anchor rode with the windless while running the engine at full throttle—to no avail. The only sensible option was to wait until the tide came up, float off, and then reset the anchor in deeper water. At least we knew what to do.

We were merrily on our way the next morning and enjoyed a smooth sail down to Charlotte Harbor, where we anchored for the night. Our first little storm occurred the following morning as we sailed towards Ft. Meyers Beach. It was nothing compared to what we had experienced in the Bahamas and it quickly passed.

Unfortunately, the troubled seas stirred up some sediment in our fuel tank and we began experiencing motor problems as we dropped sail and headed into the channel to find the anchorage. Both the fuel filers we had on hand were used up while trying to get in but we made it and safely anchored before dark. The following day, we moved *Happy Ours* into one of the marinas and set out on foot in search of more fuel filters only to find that the particular type needed were in short supply and would have to be ordered.

We enjoyed our new surroundings and quickly learned that perhaps the best part of cruising is getting acquainted with new, interesting people and places. Allen and Sharon's enthusiasm was dampened as they watched their vacation quickly slip away with no definite sailing days in site. We sadly said goodbye as they headed back to pick up their van.

As much as we enjoyed our guests, Norma and I found new freedom in having just the two of us aboard. We found it easier to make new friends and just do our own thing. We were invited to sign up for a cruise on the Big M casino boat with the understanding that once under weigh, I would be given a private tour of the engine room. Sure enough, just when I had lost my limit, my friend John, who stayed with his wife in our marina, showed up and gave me a tour. Turned out he was the engineer a couple days a week and really knew his stuff!

We finally received six new fuel filters and hung around long enough to celebrate the Fourth of July on the beach—one of those magical occasions we will always remember.

Soon, we were on our way to Key West. Waiting for good weather has its rewards: The wind and waves were perfect for sailing and the next twenty-six hours were spent in two-foot seas sailing along under close and beam reaches. The moon was full that night providing a world full of silvery, shimmering seas and we enjoyed a communion with both God and nature.

The wind started dying down and it was time to again start the motor. We furled the sails and motored along for about an hour before the contaminated fuel problem once again raised it's ugly head. We went thru half of the new filters before giving up and calling Tow Boat US. We had made it to the outer buoy and set up a rendezvous to be towed the rest of the way in. This is not how we had planned to parade in front of Sunset Pier!

Arriving in Key West undertow, *Happy Ours* was docked unceremoniously at one of the available side-to slips near the raw bar. We arranged to have the fuel polished and the two of us set off to explore our new surroundings. There was much we had missed on our previous visit with Skip and Sandra on *Win Dancer* and finding something to do while waiting for repairs wasn't difficult.

What a fun place to be broke down! We enjoyed watching the juggler at sunset pier, touring an old lighthouse, visiting Harry Truman's home away from home, and playing with the six-toed cats at Hemingway's. Our slip was in a very noisy location with different music blaring from the loudspeakers at various nearby bars. We decided if you can't beat them, it was best to join them. Food was great and drinks plentiful. We were almost sorry to have the fuel polished and be on our way but by then, the Hurricane season was in full bloom and Texas had already been hit.

We sailed around the tip of Florida and spent the night in Marathon. From there, we headed down the channel and anchored in Rodriquez, crossed the reef the next morning, and found ourselves in the Atlantic Ocean for the first time alone. Even with larger waves, sailing was great. With the help from the Gulf Stream, *Happy Ours* at times was making good 12.5 knots under sail. We spent our first night and the following day cruising along without incident, and decided to set out a bad weather forecast in St Augustine. Our cruising guide suggested getting local knowledge before entering the inlet as it is plagued with a bottom of shifting sandy shoals.

Having arrived too late to enter in daylight, the only option was to heave-too until the next morning. The foul weather started moving in around three AM and by daylight, we were anxious to go in. Contacting Tow Boat US, we were told to hug the red buoy as we entered the bay and the marina was to the left. When we headed in, we found the waves to be larger than anticipated and we passed the red buoy sliding sideways, nearly out of control, on a wave's crest. As soon as we cleared the breakwater, the engine's power took over and quickly propelled us up to the fuel dock of the marina.

We fueled up, took on water, and rented a slip for the night to get some much-needed sleep; however, St Augustine is the oldest city in the U.S. and needed to be explored. Upon awakening, we took in the local sites and even drank from the fountain of youth— We held our nose, closed our eyes, and took a drink! It tasted really bad and we're still waiting for results.

The weather settled the second day and we headed back out to play in the Gulf Stream. In a couple of days, the weather started deteriorating with rainsqualls and strong gusty winds, which eventually swung around to the Northeast. With the Gulf Stream current heading North and the winds coming out of the Northeast, the seas turned into giant square waves with white foam spewing off the tops in the thirty-five knot winds. The deafening sounds of the wind screaming in the rigging and the incessant banging of the waves slamming into *Happy Ours'* hull did more than un-nerve us.

In all the noise, a fresh water hose burst at the hot water heater and the entire contents of our 195—gallon water tank pumped overboard with out our noticing. We still had some bottled drinking water but how could this have happened? Lesson learned—turn the water pressure pump off while under weigh or when leaving the boat!

Checking the charts, we decided to sail into Beaufort, SC. It was a long ways in from where we were; however, by falling off and reaching under sail, we were able to make it just before the marina closed at 5p.m. The dock master helped secure our lines and when the paperwork was finished, he headed home. A large sport fisherman came in just behind us and when they landed, one of the crew jumped off and literally kissed the dock. They too were glad to be in.

Finding food that evening led us to finding some new friends—Joe and Sandy Pots. They were on a very comfortable powerboat named *Brandy*, which was in a slip at the marina and they too were heading north. Joe was a member of the Coast Guard Auxiliary and we spent several hours comparing his training with ours in the Power Squadron, coming to the conclusion that the classes were very similar.

We toured the town together and spent many happy hours simply just enjoying each other's company until it was time for us to leave. Joe told us that Sandy refused to go out into the ocean, and presented the idea we might travel together on the Intercostals Waterway. He was very familiar with the ICW and was willing to share his knowledge.

Things such as timing bridge openings as well as being able to pick out the deepest water in a muddy channel were foreign to us—much different from sailing in the open ocean. The prospect of learning new skills swayed us into trying the ICW.

Motoring along day after day, observing all the beauty that the east coast of the US has to offer was worth the fuel cost. Beautiful expensive homes with perfectly groomed lawns passed by, sometimes giving way to farmland or lush green woods. Each night, we either anchored out or found a marina in some historic place and enjoyed exploring what we had only previously read about.

We arrived at historic Charleston harbor on July 26, 2001 and found slips at the municipal marina. This place was a history buff's delight. We were reminded that the first shot of the Civil War was fired here at Ft Sumter!

Culinary delights such as our first soft-shell crab sandwich, shrimp and grits, Shepard's pie, and real crab cakes, alone made the trip worth doing. We ate our way thru Wilmington, Georgetown, and Morehead City. On August 15, 2001, we reached Columbia, NC, and had completed nearly 1200 nm of our trip. Mile marker eighty-four was a decision point and the four of us put in at the Alligator River Marina to rest and catch up on email.

Joe discussed going thru the Dismal Swamp Canal, an old logging canal built in George Washington's time. We questioned whether *Happy Ours* with her nearly 6' draft would make it. I called the canal office and was told they had just spent over a million dollars to renew the canal and I should have no problem locking thru. The decision was made!

Norma and I enjoyed hoisting sail and cruising thru the Albemarle Sound in moderate wind and seas only to watch our friends on their power boat getting beat up in the same conditions. Joe called on the VHF radio and announced they were tired of all the bouncing around and was going to throttle up and get to the destination in a hurry. We met them at Elizabeth City, where we spent the night and where we staged for entering the first lock in the morning.

Getting up early, we made it to the lock a little ahead of time and dropped anchor to wait for the signal to enter. Joe went first, putting sufficient fenders out to keep his boat well off the concrete wall of the lock and prepared two long lines to control the position of their boat as the lock flooded. We followed, doing the same. As soon as we entered, a gate was shut behind us and the water began to rise. When we reached the top, I stepped off a moment to visit with the old worn and weathered lock tender. He asked how much *Happy Ours* drew and about her other dimensions. Finally he put his hand on my shoulder and told me that I'd be fine if I did everything he was going to suggest. This did not give me a warm and fuzzy feeling!

Luckily, there was no traffic heading south on the canal, so we were directed to stay in the middle of the channel all the way. His advice worked well, we only touched bottom once or twice without incident. Joe's twin screws were kicking up some old waterlogged timber and we heard them thump the hull a time or two. This was remedied by putting more distance between us and by slowing down a little.

The canal was similar to a river, with long straight stretches of water, lined on both sides with thick green trees that curved out over it, forming an uncompleted arch. There was a place to tie up and spend the night along the way; however, we chose to continue on and tie up at the far end in preparation for an early lock opening the next morning.

To our horror, a beaver had fallen a tree large enough to span half the width of the canal. I steered carefully around the obstruction, as our friends on *Brandy* had done, nervously watching the depth gage. I was relieved to note that there was plenty of water under us but failed to consider the thick tree limbs that curved out from the bank.

Ka-whack; Our 60 foot tall mast struck an overhanging tree limb, causing *Happy Ours* bow to climb into the air while hundreds of small tree limbs and leaves rained down upon us. The deck was covered and the dink on its davits was full. *Happy Ours* was camouflaged for jungle warfare! The bow slowly dropped and our speed resumed as we headed back to the center of the canal.

Norma took the helm and I went on deck to inspect for damage and clear the debris. Nothing was really hurt; however, we were going to have to enter Norfolk with a ridiculous tree branch sticking up proudly from the top of our mast. Try as I would, nothing could entice it to come off.

We spent that evening sharing a small dock at the lock with our friends. Several restaurants were within walking distance, and we had no trouble finding one to our liking. The next morning, we locked thru and the scenery changed from quiet, tree-covered banks to the very busy waters of Norfolk. Our first task was to dodge a giant container ship and then arrange for a bridge opening. We felt as green as the tree flying at our masthead as we gawked around at all of the large ships, both military and commercial. It seemed to take no time at all to arrive at our marina and get settled in.

The new Grunert cold plate refrigeration system that we had installed before leaving Palmetto was failing and needed immediate attention. The dock master found us a repairman for the following day, so we were free to remove the unsightly tree limb and explore the town.

Restaurants were plentiful and there was much to see and do. Macarthur's museum was one place we enjoyed as well as touring various waterfront attractions. The town was Navy all the way, populated with people whose entire family worked in the shipyards and the military families of those who served on the ships. Nearly anyone on the street could tell of the coming and going of the ships and spoke of them as if they were members of their own family. Pride was displayed everywhere we went and it was infectious.

The problem with our refrigerator was severe, and a whole new compressor and plates was placed on order. It turned out one of the existing plates that we re-used on the advice of the Florida Dealer had an internal leak, which destroyed our new compressor and contaminated the entire system with ethylene glycol.

Our repairman arranged for us to move *Happy Ours* to neighboring Portsmouth to a slip in the new marina where his shop was located. They waived the marina fees and provided electricity and water free, which helped us bear the cost of replacing the refrigerator. Joe and Sandy could wait no longer and had to move on. We sadly said our goodbyes and vowed to keep in touch.

The refrigerator was replaced in another week, and it was time to head for the Potomac, our next destination. On September 11, 2001, I walked into the marina office early to check out and arrange to top off our fuel tank only to find the dock master glued to his TV. He hardly acknowledged my presents, and so I walked over beside him to see what he was watching. It looked like a movie with fire pouring out of a tall building—just then an airplane crashed into the side of another building. He gasps and told me it was no joke, that this was the twin tower under attack. We stood there together, watching the news unfold. I forgot about the checkout and returned to *Happy Ours* to tell Norma to turn on the TV.

The dock master came to tell us not to leave and that no fuel could be sold at the present time. The bridge to Washington DC was locked down and the Potomac was no place to be.

Norfolk had come alive and there were military patrol boats with mounted machine guns running up and down the Elizabeth River, guarding the shipyards. Some strange looking military vessels were making their way down the river and heading out to sea and the VHF radio was a buzz with the military announcing that all civilian vessels were to stay more than 100 yards from commercial ships and military vessels.

With no fuel available, we were invited to stay in the marina another week at no cost, which was a relief because our whole country was on alert and we really didn't know where to go. Norma silently wept as she watched one of the war ships heading down the river with the proud, brave crew dressed in whites, standing in formation on its deck.

One morning as we sat in the cockpit, a giant shadow overtook us, even though there was not a cloud in the sky. When we looked around, we saw the mammoth Harry S Truman aircraft carrier moving quietly past. It was so big, it literally blocked out the morning sun and we watched in amazement as she slipped out of sight. The sky was filled with nothing but war birds and we could only speculate what the future would be; however, even in all this gloom and uncertainty, the mood lightened up some as a Disney cruise ship came in to dock for repairs and piped the tune to "When You Wish Upon A Star" on its horn as it was tying up.

Finally, in about a week, we were allowed to fuel up and head out. Our plans had once again changed, and we motored past Hampton Rhodes and headed up the Chesapeake. Our goal was to reach Annapolis in time for the big annual sailboat show. It was just the two of us now and we hoisted sail as we left the busy shipping lanes behind and settled into the wonderful life of cruising in the Chesapeake. Sailing there was very pleasant, with nearly calm seas and a steady wind.

Of all the anchorages in the Chesapeake, one stands out the most in our memory: Tangier Island. With our bow pulpit still smarting from the fateful trip into Venice a long time ago, we decided to forget fighting a three knot crosscurrent into a slip and opted to obtain permission to tie up at the fuel dock for the night.

As soon as our lines were secured, we hopped off onto the dock and immediately were shocked to come face to face with the dock master. At the risk of being rude, we both stared into the most unusual set of blue eyes the likes of which we had seen only once before. He had the eyes of Norma's father, Arnold Park. We were a long ways from Arnold's farm in Missouri and were fascinated to learn that this fellow was also named Park.

Tangier Island is a special place forgotten by time. Most of the houses are small and old but well kept. Crabbing is the main source of income and the shore is lined with hundreds of well-maintained, small white fishing boats. The people are religious and friendly and seem to speak English with a very old sounding and strange accent.

Walking along the small streets on the island revealed a young man on a bicycle with those same blue eyes, and on down the path was an old cemetery dating from the 1600's, with three predominant names on the tombstones: Crockett, Park, and Pruett. These had to be some of Norma's ancestors.

That evening we dinned on delicious blue crab claws in one of the local restaurants—another new experience. We were furnished a wooden hammer with which we were supposed to crack the claws. Norma gave her first one a whack and nothing happened. Being the determined soul she is, the second whack was much harder, breaking the little hammer and sending its head flying across the room. The waitress came over with a new hammer and showed us how to strike the back of a knife blade held firmly on the claw in order to crack it. Norma did this and it worked like a champ. "Where are you two from," the waitress asked with a smile. When Norma told her "Kansas City," she just nodded and told us we were the first she had met from there.

Our next stop was the Solomon Islands, which have their own special charm. We especially enjoyed the lighthouse museum. Only forty-five nm left to get to the boat show!

We arrived in Annapolis the day before the boat show was to begin. Because of all the delays and change of plans, we were much later than anticipated and found all the anchorages full. One marina had some expensive slips available, so we rented one for a week, not wanting to miss any of the show.

I can remember flying to Annapolis and enjoying the show once before. We stood on the docks, looking out over the anchorage at all the sailboats and promised ourselves to return by boat some day. This was truly a dream come true!

The show offered several seminars on topics of interest to sailors and we signed up for every possible one of them. Tents were set up all around and venders offered discounts and information on their various wares. Every dock featured beautiful new boats to explore and dream about.

We purchased a new nine-foot Caribe hard-bottomed dink and a 9.8hp motor to replace the Avon roll up that came with the boat as well as an Iridium Satellite phone for emergency communications.

The SSCA was on hand with their own social and seminar to add to the fun and fellowship. We even ran into Rich and Bobbie on *Hideaway*, our mentors from the leeward island trip several years ago.

Greg and Sandy Dostal (friends from the St Louis Power Squadron) were wandering around on the docks to our surprise and delight. We invited them stay on *Happy Ours* for the week and they, in turn, provided not only the use of their car but also hours of hilarious fun.

We didn't stay long after the show ended—it was getting cold and it was time to head south for the Bahamas. We hoisted sail and literally got in line as white sails headed south dotted the skyline for as far as we could see. Anchoring room was at a premium each night; however, the spacious Chesapeake managed to accommodate us all.

We navigated the ICW on the way south, via Coinjock, the Alligator River, Belhaven, Oriental, Morehead City, Charleston Harbor, Beaufort, Sc, Hilton head, and Savanna.

Savanna is historically similar to Charleston except there is much more of it. The town is divided into small communities surrounding a series of parks that they call squares. Each square has a focal point fountain or monument and all are well kept. Surrounding the squares are beautiful old homes, which display at least three periods of architecture. Norma liked the Victorians best.

My favorite part was the waterfront, with its cobblestone streets, interesting shops, and of course, seafood restaurants. The Pirate House is a famous restaurant—a place Black Beard often stayed and there is a tunnel running from here to the docks thru which men were often kidnapped and taken for crew.

Just to prove that we were still very much Missourians, we walked the waterfront in search of the old Savanna light. Turned out that we had stood under it several times. It didn't resemble a lighthouse at all, but was an old ornamental street light standing tall in a park overlooking the Savanna River.

At Norma's insistence, we allowed ourselves one Victorian House Tour—the birthplace of Juliet Gordon Low, founder of the Girl Scouts.

The ICW proved not foolproof during foul weather—a late season hurricane was just five hundred miles off shore, causing heavy rains and wind-driven tides high enough that the banks overflowed, leaving only tall grass sticking up out of the water to steer by.

After an exhausting day piloting in these conditions, we spotted a fairly large sailboat high and dry, lying on her side. Wind had increased throughout the day and it was time to seek the safety of an anchorage. We found an unnamed creek on the charts and carefully eased *Happy Ours* in. After several futile attempts to set our anchor, (each time the howling wind would pull it out immediately), I had Norma hit the bow thruster as soon as I had dropped our primary anchor. The bow quickly fell off with the power of the thruster. I guessed at what forty-five degrees might be, released the second anchor and played out both Rhoades at the same time, setting both anchors simultaneously. *Happy Ours* smartly came up into the wind and stayed put.

We spent five days here and found ourselves surrounded by seven other yachts, all anchored in this little creek before the storm died down. There was absolutely nothing to do except periodically check the ground tackle for chafing and listen to the howling wind. This was a new experience for us and once the initial worry passed, we each found a novel, propped up our feet and read. Reading helped us relax and kept our minds off the weather.

As soon as the wind died down, we escaped and headed south, stopping at Jekyll Island, and then out of St Augustine inlet into the Atlantic for a much-needed sail. We went back in at Cape Canaveral inlet, then down the Indian River. It was early December, and we decided to leave *Happy Ours* at Whitley Marine, rent a car, and drive to KC for the Holidays. Icy roads, snow and foul weather made the trip home a challenge and we vowed to spend our winters south from then on.

On arriving back at Whitley marine in Cocoa, Fl we were treated to witnessing a space shuttle launch. (I have never seen anything so spectacular!) The vibrations were so strong that they could be felt as rumblings in our chest and the world seemingly illuminated with light nearly as bright as the sun. All watched in awe as the huge monster gracefully lifted itself, as if in slow motion, towards the heavens and slipped silently out of sight.

We spent New Years Eve celebrating with friends—then it was time to provision up and head for Lake Worth, our jump off spot for the Bahamas. Saying goodbye, we eased back up the Indian River and out of the Canaveral inlet into the Atlantic Ocean, which seemed to be waiting for us. Seas were a little rough but the wind was friendly and *Happy Ours* cruised along under sail nearly all the way to Lake Worth inlet.

The weight of our new dink proved too much for the davits in rough seas and one of the welds broke and needed repaired and braced. I took the davits to a local welder in one of the marinas by dink and he promised to have them ready to go before closing. The weather was perfect for a night crossing of the Gulf Stream and we didn't want to miss the chance.

At five p.m the davits were ready as promised, allowing some daylight for re-installing them and mounting the dink. That being done, we ate supper, celebrated with a glass of wine, and waited excitedly for the proper time to weigh anchor.

Neither of us could sleep and we busied ourselves by pouring over charts and cruising guides and re-planning our crossing. Most of the literature advised sailing more to the south, letting the current bring you back in line to make landfall at the west end. That's what we opted for. It took only ten hours to get to the west end—all under motor in calm seas and no wind.

Chapter 8

Back to the Bahamas

When we left out of Lake Worth the sky was beautifully decorated with bright, twinkling stars and there was absolutely no wind. Dodging the highly illuminated dredges at the mouth of the harbor, we eased out into the Atlantic heading southwest to allow for the strong Gulf Stream current.

Taking turns standing watch allowed each of us to doze as we watched the autopilot steer from waypoint to waypoint. We were leaving the US waters for the first time on our own and to say we were excited would be an understatement.

The first time we had crossed the Gulf Stream had been on *Wind Dancer*, heading the other way. This was different. There was no Skip and Sandra with whom to share the experience—just the two of us with the sole responsibility of our own safety. We carefully tracked our course and it was easy to determine when we had arrived in the strong, un- relenting current of the Gulf Stream. The autopilot pointed our bow more south even though we wanted to go east.

Increasing the engine's rpm helped us to maintain the course made good and we realized our trip could have been shorter and quicker had we only entered a waypoint for the West End and just increased speed as needed. Under sail would have been a different story; however, experience is the best teacher. Around 4 a.m., I could hold out no longer and woke Norma to take the helm, setting the stage for Norma to make our first landfall!

It is best described in her words:

When Bob woke me, it was still dark. The autopilot was working fine and I huddled up in the front of the cockpit under the dodger, looking out over the dark water. For a long time, there was really nothing to see and I just sat there, trying to stay awake. After a while, little flickers of morning light with hues of beautiful pinks, yellows and blues started appearing in the sky. There were no other boats to be seen and I imagined seeing trees on the horizon in front of us. As they grew taller, the trees turned into clouds in the sky creating the strange illusion that we were going down hill towards them. Soon the island appeared, first as a gray shadow, and then I thought I could see some buildings. This was one of the most exciting moments of my life and I woke up Bob to share it with.

At the West End, Bahamas we were instructed to pull along side a tall concrete wall where we met with friendly officials who checked us in to their country. Deciding to spend the night in the adjacent marina, as the holding was considered poor in the anchorage, we slept very sound after having made our first landfall.

The following morning greeted us with bright sunshine pouring in the hatch above our heads as if to announce the picture perfect weather. Under weigh early, we headed north in search of the deepest part of the cut leading into the Northern Abacos. Having never sailed in this part of the Bahamas kept us on alert as we left the deep blue water behind and faced the more greenish white world that lay ahead.

We spent that night anchored behind Great Sale Cay, enjoying the peaceful solitude and beautiful sunset— having spent the entire day under easy sail had already mellowed us and this was just icing on the cake! We awoke to another beautiful day and headed out under sail. We sailed until it was time to turn into the wind and negotiate a fairly narrow channel at which time we dropped sail and started the motor. It ran smoothly for about twenty minutes, and then the temperature alarm sounded. A quick check of our wet exhaust revealed no water flow and we quickly shut the motor down and rolled out the main sail. Norma tacked thru the channel while I replaced the raw water pump impeller. The engine was hot and uncomfortable to work on but we had it purring again in about an hour.

Anchoring at Manjack Cay, we spent the evening taking in all the magic that surrounded us. We had passed many beautiful little islands and realized how difficult it was to pick and choose between them. The northern Abacos seem nearly untouched and isolated compared to the sometimes-crowded anchorages of the South.

Waiting for good light, the next morning found us negotiating the narrow, shallow channel at Green Turtle Cay. We dinked ashore and visited The Albert Lowe Museum, ate some conk, and topped off our supplies. Having been here once on the Wind Dancer, we were quickly ready to move on and began studying the weather for a window to safely transit the dreaded Whale Cay cut.

With north or east winds, the surging current sets up a rage. Many boats have been dashed upon the rocks and we learned that a catamaran had been lost here the previous day. I remembered when we passed through before; Skip was running his engine full throttle and was only making good about three knots in moderate conditions.

We listened intently to the radio for advice and soon it was time to try it. It reminded us of being in a parade as boats of various flags and descriptions headed for the channel to take advantage of the favorable forecast.

To our delight, all went well and the beautiful Bahamas sun illuminated the relieved smiles on all our faces as most of us dropped anchor to explore the beautiful Great Guana Cay. We downed some Guana Grabbers in honor of Jim and Helen McMullen, with whom we had first shared these drinks many years ago and enjoyed more conk dishes.

Our next destination was Marsh Harbor where we picked up some Power Squadron friends (Jerry and Betty Branscum) from Kansas City. They spent a wonderful week with us just hanging out. We sailed most every day, ate conk in about every form imaginable, and spent Valentines day at the Guana beach resort enjoying a steak, lobster, and shrimp dinner topped off with desert.

Jerry and Betty flew home and we started watching for a weather window to head south—Georgetown race week was just around the corner. We left Marsh Harbor, anchored at Lanyard Key, sailed thru Little Harbor cut, spent a crowded night anchored at

Royal Island, transited current cut, then on to Hatchet Bay, Rock Sound, and Georgetown in the Exumas. Sailing was good and the weather pleasant the whole trip.

A thing of interest, yet unexplained to us, occurred while we were anchored at Lanyard Key. It was a dark night with nearly no moonlight. Far from city lights, the sky was lit up with some of the brightest stars that we had ever seen. Some were being reflected in the calm, dark water and we were commenting about it when, to our surprise, we noticed a bright green light blinking in the water below. For about an hour we watch as hundreds of these things surrounded the boat with their dazzling green flashes reminding us of the lighting bugs that populated the yards and fields at night in Missouri. What a beautiful night!

George Town race week was all that had been promised. Nearly four hundred boats were in attendance and we found many cruising friends were there to share the fun. It was a surprise to see John and Amanda on *Gingi*, whom we had met in Norfolk. They had become special friends and we, once again spent some good times together.

We attended beach parties, pig roast, bonfires, talent contest, dink races, boat races, dances under the stars, and were even entertained by an Irish singer on St Pat's day. Some times in the early evening, John would play his trumpet, filling the anchorage with the sounds of his beautiful music.

As a special treat Eileen Quinn performed a concert, entertaining us with songs about the sailing life. Not knowing originally who she was, we were very surprised when this delightful person with whom we had visited all week, got up from the table and started singing. We purchased one of her CD's and had her autograph it—a priceless possession. The only thing that bothered me was that Norma would play one of her songs over and over: *Who Would Know if I Killed the Captain.*

Leaving Georgetown, a windy sail led us to Conception Island where we explored a narrow white sand beach. It is said that Columbus landed here and had probably walked on the same sand. From Conception, an overnighter put us at Myaguana. It was raining there so badly that we just anchored on the outside and left for

Provo in the Turks and Caicos that night when the weather cleared. *Happy Ours* gave us a great ride with all 3 sails up and drawing, under the bright light of a full moon. We averaged six knots while giving the motor a rest.

After a little exploring, we fueled up and headed for Luperon, in the Dominican Republic. This place is unbelievably beautiful with lush green mountains and an action-filled town. It is a wonderful change of pace from the more flat, peaceful Bahamas.

We had been warned not to pay extra money at the Commondante's office after paying a fee at immigration and sure enough, we found him with his hand out asking for a tip. I pretended not to understand Spanish and pulled out three pesos instead of the three dollars US he was asking for and dropped the coins in his hand just as some of his co-workers rounded the corner to witness the event. Making an ostentatious protest, he quickly handed me back the coins and motioned for us to leave. His friends were grinning at him and we thought we detected him blushing.

Our first night in town found us at a local watering hole where we met Bruce Van Sant, author of the popular cruising guide *The Gentleman's Guide to Passages South*. He and his beautiful wife Rosa were staying here and definitely contributed to the fun. The town itself reminded Norma of the Missouri Ozarks back in the fifties, with its open markets and laid back atmosphere.

The water in the anchorage was slime green and full of moss—not a pretty sight. Norma chose this particular harbor to fall off the dive platform while she tried to climb into the dink and disappeared under the surface only to re-appear a moment later coughing and sputtering. Her hair was entangled with long, green streamers of mossy looking stuff and her clothes had already taken on a curious looking green tint. Luckily, the only thing injured was her pride and I dared not laugh as I plucked the green monster from the depths. She immediately showered in the cockpit and began the tedious task of removing the nasty vegetation from her hair. Finally, she was clean enough to go below and take a hot water shower, using plenty of soap and shampoo. Afterwards, she gargled with Listerine, then downed a glass of wine. Things were back to normal.

While waiting for weather, we took several trips to the interior, fell in love with their Presidente Beer, enjoyed Salsa lessons and found time for some Spanish lessons as well.

The anchorage was full of yachts waiting out the weather to head south and the whole place was consumed with a party-like atmosphere. Friendships were cemented that would last for many years to come.

Taking advantage of the first weather window, we headed into town to clear out. All went well until we went to the Commondante's office. He was not there, and one of the other fellows handled our paperwork. I spoke to him in Spanish as we filled out the paperwork and before he stamped it with the official seal, he scowled at me, held out his hand and demanded three pesos!

Blinking, I looked at him in disbelief, trying to decide if I had understood him correctly. Military men in uniform surrounded us and I could see no reason to antagonize him so I reached into my pocket and placed three of the near worthless coins in his hand. All of a sudden, he and all his men broke out in good-natured laughter as he returned my coins and stamped our paperwork. They must have all had great fun catching the boss with his hand out when we arrived!

We left with a buddy boat called Sea Witch with new friends John and Deb on board as well as Dick and Susie on *Sojouner* and headed straight for Boqueron, Puerto Rico. We sailed and motor sailed for about fifty hours to get there. The trip could have been split up but we were afraid of loosing the weather window.

The Mona Passage that everyone talks about was very kind to us except for at about four a.m., when we were rounding the hourglass shoals. The shoal is really a giant hourglass shaped mountain range submerged in about a thousand feet of water. There is still plenty of depth shown on the chart to sail across it; however, in his book, Van Sant cautions that strong current and much confused energy exists in this area and that it should be avoided.

As luck would have it, a squall came up just as we were rounding the shoal. The seas were black and rolled and pitched in an unpredictable wild motion. Our speed over the ground dropped from

6.5 knots to 1.5 knots and we got to enjoy what is known as the Caribbean two-step for a while. We could see the shoal; it looked like a cauldron with white waves and foam boiling up from the ink and we were glad we had decided to sail around it. Just being near was bad enough.

Happy Ours did just fine—we powered up the engine and motored out of there as fast as we could. Sea Witch, on the other hand, was not as lucky. It's radar reflector came crashing to the deck, a fuel can broke loose, covering the aft deck with fuel, the refrigerator door flew open, dumping its contents all over the cabin and John fell, catching his ankle in the spokes of the wildly turning wheel at the helm. Thank goodness; before it could shatter his ankle, the linear drive unit on the autopilot broke instead, leaving him with only a limp and no autopilot. Dick and Sue on Sojourner were ahead of us and had very little problems.

Our arrival in Boqueron was uneventful; we cleared customs, toured the town and headed for Salinas. We arrived just in time for the sailor's Friday night barbeque. The following day Dick and Sue shared the cost of renting a car, which allowed us to visit a West Marine store in Farjado. The girls shopped till we all dropped at an outlet mall, then we visited the beautiful rain forest with its hiking trails, waterfalls, and nearly two hundred varieties of trees.

In Salinas, we celebrated our first anniversary of living aboard, having covered about 4000 nautical miles. Want to loose a year quickly? Just head out on a sailboat!

While we were there, another surprise—Skip and Sandra Kelly on *Wind Dancer* came up on the SSB radio and were in Trinidad, just finishing some work. *Hide Away* and *Starlight Dancer* weren't with them but both broke in to say hello. It had taken us years but we were now within radio range! I made a copy of a letter Norma sent to her folks; it is a refreshing change from my usual perspective. Hope you enjoy it:

"We left Luperon last week after three weeks waiting for a weather window, we traveled, 240 nm in forty-eight hours arriving in Boqueron, Puerto Rico. Today we left at five a.m. for a twelve-

hour sail to Salinas. The shoreline, lighthouses, and mountains are beautiful from the water. We will be in Salinas about a week. We have been traveling with two other couples from Illinois.

Luperon is like stepping back in time to early 1900's. They ride horses, mules, and donkeys. Growing sugar cane, pineapples, fruits, and vegetables on hilly land were a tractor couldn't go. Ladies there do laundry by hand. They butcher hogs and hang them up; selling and cutting up to what amount of pork you want to buy on the street. You want chicken; they catch it, ring its neck, scald and pluck. They hand the chicken to you head, legs, and feet for a small amount of money—Less than a dollar. They have lots of cattle, doing milking by hand. Most do not have electricity or running water. As you know, phone service is real bad. They do have some autos, their driving is as bad as their phone service. They are real friendly Spanish speaking people. Bob and I took a Spanish class but have much to improve.

Fruit we purchased in Luperon is the best we have ever eaten. Grapefruit the size of cantaloupe and so sweet you would think it had to be an orange. We did three tours in the D.R.; one was to the water falls were you could slide down the falls. Bob and I chose to watch as we didn't want to take a chance on getting hurt and not being able to travel—there were some with broken bones from going down the falls. Getting to the falls was very interesting—you need a 4-wheel drive. The last one and a half miles was on foot, wading in the water and climbing over rocks; it was just a path.

Arriving in Puerto Rico is like being back in the U.S. (Kmart, Wal-Mart, etc). As I write this, we are making 8.5 knots with sails up and motor running. Dick and Sue on Sojourner a forty-six foot 1998 Tartan is racing us. He can't stand to be last; his boat has the same motor as ours, sixty-two H.P.

Salinas was great. We went to a sailor's barbecue Friday evening. We rented a Car with Dick and Sue and saw Puerto Rico on Saturday. Got to get this in the mail as we may be leaving tomorrow. You guessed it, I loved Luperon and I am enjoying cruising life very much"

Chapter 9

A Dash to get Below 12.5

Leaving Puerto Rico, we sailed to Cuelbra in the Spanish Virgins where we spent the night, then on to Virgin Gorda. *Sojurner* broke off and went on to St John, leaving *Sea Witch* and *Happy Ours* to go it alone. *Sea Witch* was hand steering and desperately wanted to repair their autopilot, a task we were told could be accomplished in Virgin Gorda.

The passage East against the trade winds had not been an easy one. Even with *Happy Ours* sixty-two hp turbocharged engine, we saw our speed made good down to as low as 3.8 knots as we crashed against contrary currents into eight to ten foot seas and fifteen to twenty knot winds, right on our nose.

Day or night, nature seemed to challenge our progress. Our ninety-five-gallon fuel tank was drained rapidly as our consumption almost doubled. Getting fuel was difficult; most of the islands had either no fuel dock or one not safe to take our six-foot draft into. We purchased several five-gallon plastic jugs and had been taking them by dink, some times to a filling station in town, hauling them on a two wheel cart back to the dink and then by dink to the boat. Fuel quality was so poor at some of these places that we had to stop filling and empty and clean the Baja filter about every fifteen gallons.

Water was as much as sixty cents/gal for RO with the average at about twenty-five cents. Seawater quality in some of the anchorages is so poor that running the water maker was out of the question.

Thank goodness we could conserve and also had a two hundred gallon tank. Other wise, we would have been carrying water also.

We found ourselves safely in St Thomas, Virgin Islands and anchored right in front of Black beard's castle. It has an ugly old tower from which he is purported to have thrown his wives when he was displeased (A custom which maybe should be given some consideration).

The first gunfire we had heard since being near Camp Lejeune occurred while *Happy Ours* danced at anchor in the harbor as a sad story unfolded in the darkness before us. A couple of bursts from automatic weapons, followed by the loud siren of a police car alerted us that there was trouble ashore. The flashing red light from the police car could be clearly scene as it wound its way along the mountain roads to a destination slightly behind the tourist shops in town, in an area we had been advised by some locals to stay out of the previous day. A lady was shot to death as she stepped out of a Laundromat with a basket of clothes in her arms and got caught in the crossfire of a drug deal that had gone bad. The local news was in English and it was clear that this could be a dangerous place.

The seaplanes landed right behind us, and ferries scampered back and fourth much too often. Rest was at a premium; the anchorage was roily and noisy. All of this aside, we felt as though we were living in the middle of a beautiful picture post card. Everywhere we looked were green mountains dotted with colorful, well-built buildings clinging on to the mountainside for dear life. Wild cloud formations created by the heating of a land mass in the middle of the ocean surround the mountaintops and oh yes, boats. Boats were everywhere.

We took a one-dollar bus ride over to Red Hook in search of a linear drive unit for our friend's boat. The steel shaft of the unit was bent and probably gave up the ghost in the storm in the Mona Passage. They hand steered all the way here and were ready for a break. Until now, parts had been nearly non-existent. It was going to cost about eighteen hundred dollars but they were glad to pay it. When the parts arrived, we sailed to Red Hook, picked them up and installed them. John created quite a lot of curiosity as he hoisted his anchor and started circling the anchorage, a necessary step in the calibration process. There was, however, better entertainment than this!

Every morning a guy and his horse came down to the cove for a swim. It was a real show to see the man and his horse swimming together in the bay, a ritual that they both seemed to enjoy.

John soon happily led the way out of Red Hook with the new autopilot steering *Sea Witch* carefully along, then we both set sail for the Bitter End.

With the worst hopefully behind us, we planned to slow down our pace and enjoy the Islands. There should now be plenty of time to get below 12.5 degrees by July 1st (our insurance dead line for hurricane season was really June 1st but we had misread the policy). We had been very fortunate in discerning weather windows; friends were still in Luperon trying to decide when to leave. SSB radio and the weather fax machine were indispensable in helping us with our guesswork.

On June 3, 2002 we arrived in Sint Maarten safe and sound after a long, rough overnight passage. Again, the motor came in very handy as the wind was on our nose all the way.

This was the first time we had flown a French flag from our spreader. Oddly, customs didn't charge us anything for clearing in and the paper work was one page easy. After clearing in, we made a beeline for a cute sidewalk cafe, ordered a French bread and cheese plate with a couple of glasses of wonderful French wine, and it doesn't get better than this! In spite of what we have heard about the French being unfriendly, most of these people treated us very well.

We climbed up a small mountain and visited the ruins of Fort St Louis. The climb was worth it as we could see all the boats in two or three harbors. The town Marigot is beautiful. There are hundreds of places to eat and shop. We shared a taxi with friends and enjoyed a tour of the island.

John and Deb on *Sea Witch* opted to meet some friends and spend time on the nude beach on the Dutch side of the island. This not being our thing, we headed on down island with Jack and Jo on *Mystic Adventure* and Phil and Cathy on *Packet Inn*, all friends from Luperon.

Before leaving, we decided to take a tour of the island together and sure enough, the nude beach was part of it. As we climbed out of the van, the first thing we saw was two very obese ladies setting naked on barstools at the outdoor bar. It was, to me, a terrible case of eye pollution and I wondered how our friends could enjoy such sights. Without a spoken word, we all climbed back into the van and directed the driver to move on to the next attraction.

The following day found us enjoying a twenty-five nautical mile sail to St Barts. Here we tied up to a mooring, which was stern and bow secured. This was a really tight anchorage with no room to swing. The town was full of shopping and eating-places as well as mountain trails to hike. An old fort and lighthouse topped off the entertainment.

After two days, we moved on to St Kitts. This was a terrible roily anchorage, very uncomfortable. We stayed long enough to tour the island, see the rain forest, the biggest fort ever, and a sugarcane plantation.

Next, we motor sailed to Little Bay in Montserrat. Six of us hired a taxi to tour the island. What a tour! Turns out the driver lived in one of the houses destroyed by the volcano when it erupted in 1997. He took us to the ruins of a town called Plymouth, which is covered in ash. We went to what once was a first class resort. Upon entering the lobby, we waded through about 8 inches of ash, finding the swimming pool still full of water. Homes were evacuated for a two-mile radius and stand as a sad testimony as to what can happen when Mother Nature acts up. What was once home to eleven thousand people now has a population of only four thousand. The British government evacuated all who wanted to leave.

The volcano was still spitting up boulders, causing dusty clouds racing after them as they came tumbling down the mountain. There was still plenty of smoke and ash pouring out of the top and it was apparent that this was an unsafe zone—not a good place to hang around. A couple of months later, we were told that the whole side of the mountain blew out and more people were evacuated.

When we sailed from the island, the rule was to stay at least two miles from shore adjacent to the volcano. This we gladly did as the wind was blowing the ash in a huge cloud off the mountaintop out across the sea.

This ash is gray black powder about like face powder. It gets into everything and is hard to wash off. *Happy Ours* didn't need any of it on her so we were careful to avoid it; however, on the way out, a rain shower dumped some ash right on top of us and it took several years to get it all off.

Our next stop was Guadeloupe. This is a really laid back place with a storybook atmosphere. We rested here a couple of days before moving on. The seas were about eight foot, with thirty-knot wind gust when we arrived.

We put in to Fort De France, Martinique for supplies (and wine), then on to Rodney Bay, St Lucia, where *Happy Ours* got a new windlass. The old one failed in Martinique and no parts were available. It was very expensive to replace it here but the option of hauling up a sixty-pound anchor with a chain rode again did not appeal to me.

Happy Ours glided along in the company of fun friends to Williabou Bay, St Vincent; Admiralty Bay, Bequia; Charlestown Bay, Canouan; and Union Island as we stopped briefly to explore each. From there, we sailed to Tyrell Bay in Carriacou and finally, headed for Prickly Bay, Grenada where we helped Phil put *Packet In* on the hard and waved good bye as he and Cathy flew home to be with an ailing parent.

Many of the yachts we had met along the way were here waiting for weather to move on to Trinidad. We woke at three a.m. the morning after Phil left to find two large Catamarans had drug anchor in all the wind and had entangled around *Happy Ours*. Hearing someone yelling help, we looked out the portholes and all we could see was white jell coat on both sides; couldn't imagine what was going on. Scrambling on deck gave us the first unbelievable glance of what was happening. Two giant fifty-foot catamarans had drug, tangling their ground tackle and wrapped themselves around *Happy Ours*, one on each side. We all put out plenty of finders, and then went to work. I noticed that with each puff of wind, our chain anchor rode would tighten, raising one of our neighbor's pontoons out of the water and I doubted that our anchor would hold much longer. There was only one yacht anchored behind us and a jagged reef was not far behind it.

Norma grabbed our air horn and tried to give the fellow some warning and he finally came on deck, rubbing his eyes in disbelief. One of the captains took a knife, dived overboard, and was able to cut free the tangled bridals that were holding the cats together. They then used their anchor rode to pull forward and free of the mess. The other cat was able to do the same thing and they both re-anchored safely. Norma and I started the engine and backed down on our anchor to assure that it was still ok and poured a glass of wine each to help us to relax. There was no major damage to any of us and we knew that we all had been very lucky. "Honey, one of those men asked if we had an underwater torch. What do you think made him believe that we had welding equipment?" Norma asked as she sipped on her wine. Looking into her baby blue eyes, I could see that she was serious and all the pent-up stress let go and I started to laugh uncontrollably. Finally, after regaining my composure, I was able to tell her that the man was from England and what he wanted was really a waterproof flashlight. We both still chuckle about that one!

Being below 12.5 degrees, our boat insurance was again in effect as it was now officially hurricane season. I was glad that we didn't need to use it.

It was good to be able to slow down again. Sailing had been a series of wild beam reaches in twenty-knot winds and seas seven to ten feet. We had taken time to tour nearly every island we stopped at and even that was done at a quick pace.

Leisurely, we toured around Grenada, becoming familiar with this interesting place. There is an expensive college there and many of the students are from the US. There were stories about the US led invasion of this country in 1983 and how glad the students were to see our troops.

Nearly all of the locals said they were glad to be saved from the revolutionary government that had seized power illegally and most view the US as a friendly hero.

Wreckage of Cuban gun boats and other military craft was still there as a testimony to the combat and we were happy to have missed the action.

Chapter 10

Trinidad

We finally arrived in Trinidad on July 21st, 2002. The sail here from Grenada was a great overnight experience. Eighteen knot winds right on the beam, all with only four-foot seas. We had to shorten sail to avoid getting there before sun up. Pat and Tom on *Ishmael* sailed with us and we rafted up at the crowded customs dock to check in.

Skip and Sandra said Crews Inn was a great place—a definite understatement. We found ourselves surrounded by convenient food and supplies, a beautiful swimming pool, showers, phone service, transportation, and cable TV.

It had been since Marsh Harbor in the Bahamas that *Happy Ours* had seen the inside of a marina. With the air conditioners both running, Norma watched CNN on the cable TV and caught up on all the news. Many of our friends were here to greet us, and best of all, slip fees were just 40c a foot.

We started getting bids on boat repairs and teak work and planned to stay several months, thru the Carnival, so it was an ideal time to rest and repair. While we were there we had the exterior teak refinished, some new teak cabinets installed, the hull micro sanded and polished, new bottom paint, more welding on the davits, more refrigeration work, new cockpit cushions installed, new canvas cover for the dink, some fiberglass work and the name re-painted. Most all the work was reasonably priced and of good quality. The haul-out yards were efficient and helpful in Trinidad and had the capability of hauling yachts much larger than ours.

Before we hauled, a terrible thing happened. An oil tanker cleaned out its tanks much to near land and the thick, black oil came flowing into the harbor, leaving only the boats on the hard unscathed. It was the rainy season and a very heavy rain came, splashing the oil up on the boat's hulls, nearly to the gunnels. This soaked into the gel coat, leaving big black streaks that would not wash off. Trinidad furnished some detergent but it was too late—the damage was done. Our air conditioners had pulled this muck up into the intakes, causing the heat exchangers to not work properly and we knew better than to run our engines. The oil seemed to destroy the chemicals in the bottom paint as well and we waited until the tide carried most of it away before scheduling *Happy Ours* for haul out.

One of the workers, a fellow named Walker assured us that he could remove the stains by micro sanding and polishing the hull at the same time we hauled out for the bottom paint and this put our minds at ease. In just a week's time, our *Happy Ours* looked as good as new. The local air condition repair shop was no stranger to oil contamination and used chemicals to clean our system for a small fee, so everything was back to normal as we returned to our slip.

Cruisers cannot discuss Trinidad with out mentioning Jessie James. He runs a taxi service that brings boaters safely to and from carnival events, shopping areas, and various celebrations. If there is a medical problem, Jessie is on the spot, helping in any way he can. Without him, Trinidad would not have been as much fun.

He introduced us to a different culture by taking us to a service at a Hindu Temple, and helped us take part in Duvali, the festival of lights.

At Christmas time, he took us to a Children's Christmas ballet, as well as various local happenings such as Carols by candlelight on the lawn of the Prime Minister's house.

Cruise Inn had a fantastic Christmas party, with live stage entertainment and a crazy gift exchange. Other activities included the Mexican Train Dominos game every Sunday at our marina, and

Spanish lessons that were given free by Marta, one of our cruising friends.

John and Carol Hamblin, friends from Stockton Lake, flew down to join us for a while. We sailed some, ate and drank some, then flew to Tobago for a couple of days of exploring that beautiful island. Weather had deteriorated to the point that sailing there wasn't advised so our old friend Jessie James and his wife helped us with the travel arrangements.

Tobago has beautiful beaches and is definitely a tourist-pleasing destination. There is one area off its shore where the sparkling clear warm water is only waste deep for miles and has a bottom of white sand with the consistency of face powder. It felt wonderful on our feet as we waded along in it and played in the water.

No sooner had John and Carole left, we got an email from Phil and Cathy on *Packet Inn* asking if they could visit us for a week in Trinidad before launching their boat in Grenada to take it back to the US.

It was really good to see them again and we were sorry to hear that they had decided to quit cruising. Jack and Jo from *Mystic Adventure* were in our marina and the six of us made the most of the time we had to spend together.

We arranged a private sunset party at Fort George by paying the watchman to keep it open until after dark. Ft George is on top of a small mountain and affords a magnificent view overlooking the bay. There are several types of old cannon among the ruins, making this place both interesting and beautiful. Ed and Helen on *Tahlequah* joined us and the eight of us sat up our picnic meal on the benches overlooking the bay. We brought enough to share with the watchman and all of us marveled at the light show that took place before us as the big orange orb dropped below the horizon, illuminating the once white fluffy clouds with every color of a rainbow. The city lights started appearing one by one below and soon bright planets and stars joined them, dazzling us with a magical panorama of lights and darkness.

Norma and I had one remaining bottle of Cabernet Sauvignon from a case we had purchased in 1972 and chose this wonderful occasion to share it with friends and toast the beautiful sunset. Much too soon, the wine was gone and our ride appeared—it was time to return to our boats, ending this delightful experience.

A couple of weeks after Phil and Cathy left; John and Deb on *Sea Witch* contacted us. They were still in Grenada and needed to come to Trinidad for a medical procedure not available where they were. They ask if they could stay with us on *Happy Ours* and if we could help them set things up.

We were delighted to have them visit and Norma jokingly reminded John that if there were any nudity, he would have to keep it behind closed doors in the back cabin.

Quickly, we called Jessie James and he took care of everything from airport transportation to the hospital appointment. With Jessie on the job, all they needed to do was climb off the plane and all the rest was taken care of.

Everyone at Cruise Inn was glad to see them and we all enjoyed hearing about their stay in Grenada. John had taken a job doing construction and Deb was involved in volunteer work. It appeared that they were thinking of making Grenada their home.

I teased John about seeing the two obese women at the nude beach and ask if everyone looked like that. He chose to ignore me and just said that they had a wonderful time there.

Deb's medical procedure turned out ok and Jessie saw to it that they returned safely to the airport. We really enjoyed their visit and promised to visit them in Grenada.

Cruise In hosted several events during their stay and we all especially enjoyed spending evenings at the pool, sipping on refreshments from the little adjoining bar and visiting with fellow cruisers and hotel guest.

Christmas was upon us and Jessie warned all of us cruisers to be careful because crime increased this time of year. We didn't think much about it until we heard a frantic call on the VHF around nine P.M one night. We weren't sure but the voice sounded like Jo on *Mystic adventure*, just four docks away so we rushed down to see what was the problem.

The shaky voice had indeed come from Jo but everything was all right by the time we got there. Jack had taken the trash up, deposited it in the dumpster, then went to the office to use the telephone. Jo had been off the boat also and when they returned, she noticed a series of wet spots on their teak deck. Thinking that liquid had leaked from the trash bag, she sent Jack forward to get the mop while she went aft to retrieve a bucket she kept in the shower. As she reached around the shower curtain in the dark room, she felt more than normal pressure against her body from behind the curtain. Suddenly, the intruder hiding behind the curtain shoved her hard enough that she went flying backwards and hit the aft bunk, falling on to the floor. She yelled in terror for Jack who came running. The first thing he saw was the intruder climbing the companionway stairs. Jack grabbed the young athletic figure by the back of his swim trunks and held on for dear life. The young man was strong enough to drag Jack up the stairs behind him and across the cockpit. Jack never let loose even as the intruder jumped overboard, leaving Jack standing there with the fellow's swim trunks in his hand. Security was notified and in spite of a thorough search, no one was found.

Jo was really shaken up and had a couple of bruises, but was ok and we all learned to lock our boats, even in a secure marina.

We attended a Christmas Ballet put on by a local youth group, enjoyed musical entertainment ranging from the sweet sounds of a trumpet to the magical tingling of steel drums. Stage shows were sponsored at and by our marina and to my horror, I even received a lap dance from one of the scantly clad entertainers at the Cruise Inn Christmas party. I nearly spilled my wine!

After spending Christmas in Trinidad, and New Years Day attending the annual SSCA gam, we were exhausted; and needed to get out of there for a while before Carnival activities began in earnest.

We chose to head for a quiet little place called St Ann in Martinique, which provided one of the best sails we ever had --

240nm to Martinique, 85% of it was beam reaching under sail. With fifteen to twenty knot winds and six to eight foot seas, we arrived at St. Ann in just under forty hours. Everything on *Happy Ours* was working well.

Arriving before sun up, we took turns standing watch as we hove too. At first light we quietly motored into the sleepy harbor and set anchor. Soon the little white church started clanging it's bell, inviting everyone to attend service and we immediately knew that this was going to be a nice little place to enjoy piece and quiet. Nothing could have been farther from the truth!

We were awakened from our nap when a familiar voice came via the VHF radio. We answered and a whole chorus of friends greeted us and we were given check in advice and told of all the social activities that we weren't to miss.

St Ann was quite a contrast from Port of France where we anchored on our last visit here. It is a sleepy little fishing village with a fair amount of tourist shops and many places to eat and enjoy. The social life is good, with botchy ball Tuesday and Thursday on the beach. Wednesday was dominos at a local pub and then Friday was cocktails on the beach.

The beach is beautiful and a major tourist attraction. The large harbor has good holding and is adjacent to Marin, a neighboring town that has a marina with about 750 slips. There must be about a thousand boats in its harbor.

Lots of old friends were here, *Paramour, Fruity Fruits, Dawn Trader, Onyx, Sister Wind, New Passages, Evergreen Forest, Figment,* and *Concerto,* just to name a few. We counted yachts we had known from as many as 13 different countries and the party continued! We decided we could rest up in our next lifetime and set out to enjoy the fun.

Two major events had taken place on this trip, one was the Southern Cross appeared just above the horizon on the way here. First time either of us had seen it and we marveled as it sparkled in the heavens above us as we shared a kiss in celebration.

The other, we witnessed a beautiful green flash just at sun set. We were standing on a pier at St. Ann and many got to witness it. A loud cheer from the crowd followed, adding to our excitement. Up until then, we had only heard of the green flash and were beginning to doubt it existed.

For those who have not experienced seeing a green flash, it is a refraction phenomenon that occurs in the lower latitudes when the golden orb of the sun just drops below the horizon, followed by an iridescent green ray of light flashing in the sky at that spot. It is an awesome light show that only rarely occurs, lasts a few seconds and requires a crystal clear, cloudless horizon.

We made it back to Trinidad just in time for the first Taste of Carnival. We had spent four days in Rodney Bay, St Lucia hiding from heavy winds and twelve to fifteen foot swells brought about by an unusual high-pressure system.

Grabbing the first weather window, we headed strait for Carriacou, spent the night, then on to Clarks Court Bay in Grenada where our friends on *Sea Witch* had been staying. Several Bar-B-Q's later, we said goodbye to *Sea Witch* and did the overnight to Trinidad.

The ocean never ceased to provide us with fun and excitement. The sail back was wonderful with a little calmer seas and winds in the fifteen-knot range. It was still mostly an easy beam reach, even in the lee of the islands.

The bright green sparkles of phosphorescence trailed behind *Happy Ours* as she slid thru the night seas. Once, just before sunset, a group of dolphins surrounded us and played along our wake. Norma guessed there to be about 100 of them, the most we had ever seen at one time.

On another occasion, we had just gotten the dink down from the davits and were heading for customs in Carriacou when a silvery wave of small minnows came upon us, leaving several handfuls flopping around our ankles in the dink. They were small but had a large fishy smell and we quickly scooped them overboard.

On that same trip, I had just stretched out in the cockpit for a nap when an Eight-inch flying fish came aboard and smacked me right in the stomach. We chased him as he buzzed around the cockpit and finally put him safely overboard - who can sleep after that! Oh yes, I caught another barracuda on the way back; still nothing to eat from our two hundred dollar fishing outfit, but it was fun.

Our mentor, *Hide Away*, the first Island Packet 44 we had ever seen, was in Trini with us. Rich and Bobbie, her owners, were very helpful with maintenance tips and even a few spare parts.

Carnival in Trinidad starts many months ahead of the actual event. Jessie James was on hand to help us visit several steel drum camps, costume shops, and informative previews (Taste of Carnival) where we met some of the characters we would later see in the parade. We were given an explanation of the meaning of their costumes and dances, which made us, feel more a part of the experience.

At our first Taste of Carnival, we met Dave and Betty on *Tydewie*. It was a big surprise to learn their family lived in Ofallon, Missouri, not two miles from our daughter. The four of us quickly became friends and took part in all the Carnival had to offer together.

Jessie arranged for us cruisers to join a band. Our costumes weren't much, just some nifty t-shirts with artwork displaying the name *Desert Rats* inscribed across the back and a toga looking thing that draped over our shoulders. Jessie dropped us off at the fenced-in compound around eight p.m. where we enjoyed an all you can eat and drink party. We took turns smearing and decorating each other with a colorful collection of greasy paints while dancing around to the much too loud sounds of a steel band. Around five a.m., the gates to the compound opened, the band and bar were loaded onto the back of a flat bed truck, and we all followed along behind it doing a chip step in time with the music. Hundreds of these bands took to the streets simultaneously and we all paraded through the streets as we showed off our costumes all covered with greasy paint. Security was provided to keep us safe and when Jessie picked us up around ten the next morning; we each were given trash bags to wear back to the marina so no paint would damage his van's interior. What fun!

We had about enough and were glad to be heading back to our boats. Upon our arrival, we took turns hosing each other down with the water hoses at the dock, and headed for the shower. A few hours sleep revived us long enough to head back to town for the evening's activities and so the fun continued.

The judging of the various categories of costumes went on and on and we spent several evenings enjoying the colorful costumes as they were paraded across the stage. Some were very large—so large that they needed cleverly concealed wheels to help support the weight. They used lots of feathers and colorful paper to build these things and we couldn't believe watching a few being blown off the stage in a wind gust.

The entire country was consumed by Carnival and the celebration lasted for a non-stop week. We were glad to have participated once while were still able but I think once was enough for us. We wore earplugs to protect our hearing and even then the amplified music was so loud that my hearing actually shut down a time or two. With all the food and drink, that week's worth of fun probably added an extra five pounds each to our girths—something we really didn't need.

Chapter 11

On to Venezuela

Dangerous pirate activity had been reported along the coast of Venezuela and it was suggested we leave out of Trinidad, head north as far as eleven degrees north to avoid the coast, and then turn west to Los Testigos. The one hundred nautical mile passage required traveling at night in order to arrive with sufficient daylight to see and avoid some reefs at the entrance.

It had also been recommended that we travel with no lights and maintain radio silence—something that went against my Power Squadron training; however, we felt this to have merit as we were traveling alone. We both stood watch all night as a precaution and arrived safely at our destination at first light.

Anchoring in a small cove, we fell immediately asleep only to be awakened by the local authorities that boarded and inspected our boat. I found it strange that they put every one of our twelve-gauge flares to their ear and shook it vigorously. We later were told that some cruisers had purchased a steel insert that would convert their flare guns to shotguns and these guys were wise to it.

The authorities allowed us three days to enjoy this beautiful place. We marveled at the hundreds of frigate birds, pelicans and gulls that swooped around us in search of food.

The second day we watched as one of the three other cruising boats launched their dink and motored over to greet us—another new lifetime friend! Denis and his little redheaded wife Rusty on *Trinity 2* were in route back to Australia, completing their circumnavigation.

We all hit it off immediately and agreed to buddy boat to Margarita and on to Puerto La Cruz, Venezuela.

Dennis was truly from the outback and was a little rough around the edges. He hardly spoke without making a strange growling sound first and really was a connoisseur of beer. We went to a casino together and were given free cocktails. His choice was a cold beer and when he had taken his first sip, he slammed the mug down on the table and announced in a booming voice "Arrr, this taste like horse piss!" and started going on about how flat it was. You guessed it—here came the waitress and a bouncer! We didn't stay long.

We sailed first to Isla Cabagua and examined the ruins of the oldest settlement in South America, which was founded by Columbus in around 1492. An earthquake had destroyed the buildings a couple hundred years ago, leaving the foundations setting silent with small lizards and stray dogs as the only inhabitants. A little monument marked the spot, which appeared to be seldom visited.

As we were preparing to head back to our boats, a weatherworn woman and a couple of youngsters wandered up to visit. She spoke no English and desperately opened her mouth, pointing inside with her finger. Dusty was a nurse and immediately took a look. The poor lady had a severely impacted tooth and her husband was away with their boat on a fishing trip. Dusty went to their boat and fetched some painkiller and other medicine and we both found some spare milk, cereal, and treats for the kids.

The woman was overwhelmed with gratitude and motioned for us to remain until she returned, leaving the children to entertain us. When she came back, she opened a small pouch, and carefully untying the drawstrings, poured some little pearls into the palm of her hand. She insisted that Norma and Rusty each take one, clearly wanting to share her treasures with us.

Our next stop found us in Arapos, a small island paradise, where we set our anchors in about 80 ft of water and tied our sterns to a rope line furnished by a local restaurant. Thank goodness there was very little wind. The food was good; however, the snorkeling was fantastic and we spent much time enjoying the underwater sites.

Our last anchorage before arriving in Puerto La Cruz was Chimana Grande, a deep-water hide out with a small inlet, surrounded by mountains. We spent hours observing the antics of huge white baby pelicans, flapping their wings in excitement as they disappeared into the beaks of their parents to get fed. There were no less than fifteen nests nearby and the bird noise was unbelievable.

The next morning, we called on the VHF for instructions to dock at Bahia Redonda Marina in Puerto La Cruz. Not only did we hear the friendly voice of Arnaldo, the dock master, but were surprised to hear Carl and Mary Lou on *Starlight Dancer* as well. We had finally caught up with the nice couple that had sailed with Skip and Sandra several years ago. Bob and Susan on *Pipe Dream* were also there—hadn't seen them since Puerto Rico and the fun began!

Puerto La Cruz is on the north coast of Venezuela and is a boater's paradise. Two or three nice marinas are connected together by a series of canals. You can use them to dink to the various marinas as well as to grocery stores, a shopping mall, and even a marine parts store. The canals are lined with beautiful homes, reminiscent of parts of Florida. Taxies are available at the marina gates to safely pick you up and take you thru the bowery to more safe parts of town at a reasonable price.

Our marina housed a pool, some small shops and most importantly, the Ankla restaurant and bar. Roberto and Marie Elena ran the place well and it was the hub of social life in the marina. Good food and great parties were just steps away from our boats.

A young woman named Anneles was an English major at the university and agreed to set up a Spanish class for us cruisers. She originally taught class one hour a day, five days a week in the restaurant. These classes became so popular; she rented an air-conditioned condo in the marina complex and taught several levels of classes throughout each day. The price increased, but it was worth it.

One party comes to mind, it was a BBQ with all the Polar beer you could drink, all you could eat, music, dancing, a mechanical bull, and the lovely Polar girl serving beer. This was all for only ten dollars

U.S. As each of us filled up on beer, we gained in courage and climbed aboard the dreaded bull with varying degrees of success. He was a mean rascal—Norma lasted less than one second. Our friend Jack on Mystic Adventure showed up with a weather worn cowboy hat and having been a cattle rancher, confidently climbed on. You could almost hear the snorting of the bull as Jack wildly waved his hat in the air and hung on with only one hand. With every "Yah Hoo," the beast seemed to get wilder until it just stopped in frustration. Jack slid easily off the thing and quietly strolled away, his large hat sheltering the biggest grin we had ever seen on his face.

I took many pictures of the happenings in the marina and would tape the best ones on a post in the restaurant for all to enjoy. Steve on *Viva*, a professional photographer from California enjoyed these pictures and showed me how to use Photoshop to enhance my work. I was quite proud of some of the results. I thought how nifty a picture of the beautiful Polar girl posed on the bull would be and asked her if she wanted to pose. My Spanish wasn't good enough so I enlisted the help of Roberto, the owner. Turned out his English wasn't as good as I thought, and unknown to me—He asked her if she would come to our boat and pose for some private pictures!

After that, every time I would go up there for a beer, she would sneer at me and slam the beer on the counter. Her bodyguard would come up and stand beside her and glare. I finally found a better translator and asked what was wrong. We all had a good laugh and she willingly posed on the bull for us, but by then, the photographer wasn't doing a very good job.

We made this marina our home base and enjoyed sailing and exploring both inland and the beautiful out islands for nearly two years. We sailed with *Pipe Dream, Texas Reb, Mystic Adventure, Tydewie* and others many times, back to Margarita, and even as far as Bonaire and back.

Bonaire itself was nearly overshadowed by stops at the Roques and Aves, some Venezuelan out islands where the water was as clear as in Bonaire and the fish were just as beautiful. The biggest thing missing was all the restrictions that we dealt with in Bonaire.

The islands were mostly deserted and housed many beautiful, unexplored reefs. Spear fishing was legal and productive.

The Aves were home to the red-footed booby birds, and it was no problem getting close enough to take pictures. While exploring this island, we found a large whale setting high and dry on a reef. He hadn't been there long and could still be recognized. I guess that I never realized how big these creatures actually were until then. His large carcass must have blown in during a recent storm and this seemed a fitting place for him to rest.

By now, it was just *Tydewie* and *Happy Ours* traveling together and the four of us explored the outer reefs, snorkeling to our heart's content. We found it best to take both dinks in case of mechanical failure, allowing us to travel further with confidence. We would drop our dink anchors in shallow water and dive overboard to swim and enjoy the beauty of our untouched surroundings.

Arriving in Bonaire, we met up with our mentors, Skip and Sandra on *Wind Dancer*, as well as several other friends from the past. Catching up on old times was fun and the diving was great. David on Tydewie and I became dive buddies and enjoyed diving on several of the sites.

David was a professional truck driver by trade and invited Norma and me to share the rental of a truck to explore inland Bonaire with him and Betty. The terrain was known to be rough and most of the roads were unpaved—no challenge for David! We spun up and slid down wet, mountain like trails without a hitch with David chuckling all the way. We saw caves with ancient stone writings, a sacred rock believed to have strange powers, isolated beaches as well as gorgeous ocean views. There was certainly more to Bonaire than just the wonderful diving.

David and Betty chose to leave with us and sail back to Puerto La Cruz, Venezuela and we decided to sail south, and then follow along the Venezuelan coast to avoid the strong counter-current in the area. During our first night out of Bonaire, the wind strengthened out of the south, causing us to motor in strong winds. This, in tern, ate up twice as much fuel as planned so we decided to anchor at Ensenada Chichiriviche to sit out the bad weather. Since we were so near, exploring an uninhabited island group in the northwestern part of the Golfo Triste was irresistible. The trees there were so full of red ibis that they resembled heavily laden apple trees back home adding to our pleasure. After spending the night in this enchanted water wilderness, we got up early and headed for Puerto Cabello where we planned to fuel up and go on our way.

Unfortunately, Puerto Cabello is one of those places it is best to avoid because of the high incidence of crime and we had no intention of doing anything there but fueling up. Anchoring in the harbor and dinking in to check on fueling procedures, we learned that our boats were not safe being unattended in the anchorage. Furthermore, we were told that it was necessary to check in to the country before receiving any fuel and that the marina there could handle the paperwork for a small fee. It was decided that the best approach was to rent slips in the marina, check in, get fuel, spend the night and be on our way.

We checked in and made reservations to spend the night in the marina. That being done, we dinked back to our boats and headed for the fuel dock, only to find it was unattended and required navigating between two underwater boulders, setting a stern anchor, and passing a bow line to the missing fuel attendant who was then supposed to pass his long fuel hose over the bow pulpit. When the depth dropped to less than seven feet, and we could raise no one, I backed *Happy Ours* out from between the two boulders and alerted Dave of the situation. Next, I called the dock master for assistance in getting into the slip.

The plan was to back up into a position in front of the slip, drop anchor and continue backing up until even with other boats at the dock, then pass our stern lines to the boats on each side and they would drag us the rest of the way in. With plenty of fenders out, a miracle occurred and *Happy Ours* actually fit into an area half its size! David lucked out and was allowed to tie up on the end of the dock.

We were told it would be ok to go into town as long as we didn't get off the main street, allowing us to visit a grocery store and several restaurants. We met a fellow off of a large sailboat that had followed us in. His boat was too big to fit into the marina and sure enough, it was robbed while he was in town.

The marina had many bright lights illuminating the surrounding water as well as a guard on every dock armed with a sawed off stainless steel 12 gauge shotgun. Even with all of that security, we heard our guard run off some swimmers he caught trying to sneak on the dock during the night.

The following day, we jerry-jugged fuel from the pump and put it in our boats—four five gallon cans at a time (two each) until the tanks were full and then we proceeded to the dock master's office to pay our bills and check out. We were told that immigration was closed until Monday and that we would have to stay another day so we tried to make the best of it by shopping and eating out. The four of us met at a very nice restaurant for lunch, then we split up and Norma and I walked down to a park at the end of the street to look at the old fort. It was still being used by the military and was not open to tourist, so we turned around and headed back to *Happy Ours*.

Norma spotted a beautiful old building about a half block down the street from the park and we decided to go take a picture of it. When we got down there, we noticed the beautiful archway entrance had no door and that the neighborhood looked a little run down.

Just then two young men walked across the street in front of us and disappeared into the open archway, only to come out a moment later. The bigger of the two held a whiskey bottle in his hand and quickly turned it into a frightening jagged weapon by smashing it against the curb. We could tell he had practiced this because it looked like something we had seen in the movies.

The two of them headed towards us, demanding our money in Spanish. I told Norma to run and assumed a position taught to me in Karate class that presented less exposure to the weapon and yelled back in Spanish " My money." We had broken our own rule and had our credit cards with us and simply didn't intend to give them up.

Norma dropped back about six paces to give me room to work, then started screaming at the top of her lungs—something she had learned in a self defense class at home. She is a good screamer and literally screamed off the smaller of our attackers. The one with the broken bottle still remained and looked more menacing than ever. He would take a step or two off to the side of me, trying to get a clear run at Norma and I just side stepped back between them and loudly cussed him in English and Spanish. Finally I tired of this game, dropped into an attack stance and screamed for the little bugger to come on as I motioned with my fingers. By then, Norma's screams had drawn a crowd and no fewer than fifteen people were standing in the street watching, but not helping.

My plan was to kick the weapon out of his hand with a kick I had practiced many times long ago, then do what ever it took to make sure it was over. I don't know if it was the crowd or if our attacker truly felt that I was going to hurt him but finally, still holding the bottle, he put both hands to his forehead, screamed out "Loco Americanos", and ran off into an alley.

I took Norma by the hand and we walked down the street together as the crowd dispersed. One old gentleman quietly whispered, "be careful" in Spanish as he patted me on the shoulder and it was over. We went back to the marina and reported the incident—they wanted to me to go back down there with them and try to find the punk. I declined, and requested no police report be made. We just wanted to check out of there and be on our way ASAP.

Clearing out went smoothly and in no time at all, we were anchoring in a little bay called Ensenada Cata. Not wanting more adventure for a while, we stayed on our boats that night and was gone early the next morning. The Venezuelan coast is beautiful with little villages on shore back dropped by tall mountains and lush green forest and we spent the day motor sailing along, listening to music and watching the villages appear and disappear from sight as we followed the coast to the next destination.

Pulling into Punta Caraballeda fifty miles later, we all did a double take, seeing a small harbor full of big, expensive power yachts and sport fishermen. The marina was full; however, we obtained permission to anchor off to the side for the night. The four of us spotted a small canal as we dinked back to our boats and decided to explore it. It was completely full of more fancy powerboats and it was clear that this was not the normal poor man's harbor. Miami would have been proud to have boats such as these in its marinas.

Our next coastal stop was Cabo Codera, a safe, hidden little anchorage with a small Catholic shrine, apparently built by fisherman to obtain the blessings and protection of Deity. We were just around the corner from Carenaro, a busy harbor with oil tanks dotting its skyline.

Codera was used as a hideout for pirates in the old days who would anchor in this secluded place undetected and wait for ships to come out of Carenero. We could almost imagine the lookout standing up on the point signaling the pirates when to attack the unsuspecting cargo vessels leaving the mainland.

For us there were no pirates; however, just at dusk several boatloads of fishermen set out nets behind where we were anchored, and left for the night. Our plan was to leave at four a.m. in order to make landfall at a low-lying island named Piritue, about eighty miles away. At four am, I could hear the anchor chain clanking as *Tydewie* got underway and we quickly followed suit. Still dark, we couldn't see where the nets were and really didn't want to foul our prop with one of them. I plugged in a search light up on the bow and swung an arc back and fourth while Norma slowly motored out of the bay. Unfortunately, the light attracted insects, which in turn attracted swarms of black bats that circled my head and body. I could feel the tickling sensation as their wings whispered against my shirtless flesh and I silently screamed in horror. Quickly dousing the light, I hit the deck and crawled back to the safety of the cockpit while Norma continued our exit at a slow pace. She had seen the terrible swarm of bats flying around me in the light and was glad to get out of there. We had heard stories of fellow cruisers being attacked and bitten by vampire bats on a near-by island and neither of us was willing to give blood!

Soon we were clear of the nets and set sail for our next destination. The sail went well and even though we couldn't see the low-lying island from a distance, our GPS directed us right to the correct spot to anchor. We had some daylight left and used it to dink ashore and explore.

The following day, there was plenty of time to dodge the monstrous oil tankers and find our way back into Puerto La Cruz where the friendly voice of Arnaldo greeted us on the VHF and gave us docking instructions, once again.

It was really good to be back and soon we were with friends, having a cold one in the marina's restaurant. To our surprise, word of the attack in Puerto Cabello preceded us and there were many unkind comments from fellow cruisers, speculating that it would have been wiser to hand over our wallets. I was starting to feel badly about deciding to fight for what was ours and had listened to about enough of the second-guessing when a stranger came up to our table.

"Are you the blokes on *Happy Ours*?"

"Who's asking?" I said, standing up from the table and looking the fellow in the eye. He said he was from England, introduced himself and his wife as fellow cruisers and stated that he just wanted to shake my hand. He said it was a pleasure to meet someone willing to stand up for themselves and when he extended his hand in friendship, I noticed some strange scars on his forearm. When I asked about them, we sat in stunned silence as we listened to their story and I was certainly honored to shake his hand. It turned out that he and his wife were anchored off the coast of Venezuela one night and were boarded by three men. When the first one came down the companionway, our new friend had shoved a hatch board full force just under his nose, causing the robber to flee, screaming out in pain. The second one met a similar bloody fate, while the third one came below with what looked like a pipe. Our friend grabbed it, only to find that it was a shotgun. It went off, wounding him in the arm and leg but he still managed to beat off the attacker. The humiliated bandits left in the middle of the night with the idea that cruisers weren't easy pray, while our friends dinked ashore in search of medical help. He was severely wounded and was bleeding profusely.

The locals were friendly and helped them get to the hospital and also guarded their boat until they could return.

In retrospect, we found that neither of us would have done anything different. Each event is unique and Norma and I don't feel it is right to second-guess someone's actions while they have faced real danger, especially if you yourself have never been forced to make such a decision.

Chapter 12

Inland Travel from Venezuela

Knowing the marina to be a safe place, we left *Happy Ours* in Arnaldo's care and enjoyed inland travel. Venezuela is a beautiful country and offered many breathtaking things to see and do. Our friend and travel agent Himey took a small group of us first to Caracas, and then on to Colonial Trovar, a tiny German village tucked away in the mountains. Long ago, a boatload of Germans had immigrated here and remained silently unknown by the government for nearly fifty years. It was a beautiful little place with German styled architecture and smiling happy people, traditional beer, sausage, and hospitality.

We stayed at a quaint little hotel up in the mountains and enjoyed the view of a little white church with a tall steeple located in the valley below. The cool temperature was a blessing to our sun-scorched skin and we enjoyed the unusual change of pace. The balcony of our hotel was surrounded by beautiful flowers and was home to colorful butterflies and iridescent blue-green hummingbirds that darted about the gardens.

I asked Himey why there was no traditional German food on the menu at our hotel's restaurant only to find out that the Venezuelan tourist didn't like it. The owner came to me and offered to prepare a special German style feast and serve it family style if everyone in our group agreed to take part. A very reasonable price was negotiated with Himey's help and the following evening we all sat down to a scrumptious meal of schnitzel, spaetzle, gravy, red cabbage and a wonderful Christmas desert basket full of several varieties of delicious cookies. Cold bottles of the local beer were served to wash the meal down and coffee or tea came afterwards. The manager and kitchen help were in a delightful mood and I suspected we weren't the only ones enjoying this special meal.

When we returned to Puerto La Cruz, an enterprising fellow named Charlie Alpha helped us explore a local coffee plantation as well as many of the near-by attractions. He worked in a travel agency in the marina complex and never missed a good party.

We booked a trip to Angel Falls, just Norma and myself for a change. We left *Happy Ours* in the marina and took a bus inland to Ciudad Bolivar. After seeing our first glimpse of the famous Orinoco River (the one that Enya sings about) we found our hotel and spent the night. Next morning we boarded a small plane and flew across the jungle to Canaima National Park where our Guide David met us. He took us up a jungle trail by Jeep until the trail disappeared into the swift current of a tannic colored river.

Here, we boarded a dugout canoe and proceeded up the river to our jungle camp where we were shown to our cabana. This camp was beautiful and resembled what we saw in the movie Fantasy Island. It provided exotic birds, plants, flowers, small waterfalls, and very important to me—clean beds, modem plumbing, and a lounge. Included in the price were three wholesome meals a day, which were as good as any we had had since leaving the U.S.

After lunch, we were taken to nearby Salto El Sapo, which is a strong, beautiful waterfall. Hanging on to a large rope, we followed a path under the thundering roar of the falls and came out on the other side for yet another spectacular view of the raging river with its lush green surroundings. Wet just don't describe what you feel when passing under all that water; it is an unforgettable experience.

That evening, we showered and headed for the Indian village for some shopping and fun. They make every thing from baskets to blowguns and there are semi tame monkeys wandering around to entertain. Norma found a nifty woven basket to purchase and while we were negotiating the price, a sharp thud occurred just to my left side. I looked up to find one of the tourists had blown into a blowgun, not knowing it was loaded—a very close call!

A good night's sleep back at the camp and a quick breakfast of ham, eggs, pancakes and coffee prepared us for the next exciting events. This time we loaded enough clothing and supplies for an overnight stay in the jungle. After about forty-five minutes, the captain of the canoe put us ashore explaining that the rapids were too shallow and dangerous for a fully loaded canoe. We walked across a sandy trail in awe of the breathtaking view. It only took thirty minutes or so and stretching our legs felt good. Along the trail, our guide pointed to a small flat-topped mountain and stated that it had been declared to be the geographical center of the earth.

Rejoining the captain on the other side, we continued for three more hours up river; getting soaked in the rapids which seemed to lurk behind every bend. Steep mountains towered over us with eerie gray clouds pouring from their tops. Rain showers could be seen in the distance as they crossed by in front of us but only the spray from our outboard driven canoe moistened us. We took a half hour rest about halfway to the jungle camp to play in a small waterfall with a pool, a definite photo opportunity.

The rapids became stronger and more frequent and the tea colored, tannic water was decorated more and more with white foam when, rounding a bend, the magnificent Angel Falls came into view for the first time. It is said to be the tallest waterfall in the world and we all sat silent, admiring the towering sight.

Shortly the captain eased our canoe onto a rocky bank and we climbed out, stumbling over the round, water smoothed rocks. Here we ate wonderful sandwiches that had been prepared ahead of time and kept in a cooler.

After lunch, we started a very rigorous climb that lasted about an hour. The trail was steep and rocky and covered with roots and slippery moss. I'm not sure how high we went but when we finished with the last nearly vertical fifty feet, we were winded. Our hot, red faces lit up the rain forest; however, with the spectacular view of the falls, and the valley below, it all seemed worthwhile. The falls still towered above and the wind blew a cool mist, creating a sort of air-conditioning as it blew over our tired, aching bodies. Picture taking was at its best. Lingering here for a couple of hours, found some of us stretched out on a rock for a nap. When you are that exhausted, flat limestone feels like a Sealy!

    The trip down was slippery and Norma fell, hitting her head on a tree root. She being determined as anybody got up, explored the new knot on her head and continued on like a trooper. There was our guide; four men and one woman in our group and by the end of this day three had fallen with no serious injuries.

    The dugout was waiting to take us across the river to the jungle camp where we were to spend the night and we crossed silently, exhausted by the day's events. I had worn an old sleeveless t-shirt that day which was inscribed with "Bushidokan," my old karate discipline, across the top, and several times our guide inquired about it. I learned that his brother was a national champ and his whole family was involved in the martial arts. He kept talking about karate and invited me to spar with him when we returned to the bottom of the mountain that evening. I reluctantly agreed, thinking that he would forget about it by then; however, that was not going to happen.

    Upon our arrival to the other side of the river, we all were led to the chicken hut like sleeping quarters where our stuff was stored and were instructed to get our towels, soap and a change of clothes and meet down at a bend in the river.

    When we returned to the riverbank, our guide was there with a curious gleam in his eye, and I could see that he had not forgotten my promise. With the rapidly flowing water as a backdrop, we positioned our bare feet on the sandy bank, bowed to each other and prepared for combat.

    He crouched down and came swirling at me like a crazed monkey, making sounds that would have made an ape blush! I had seen this style before and knew he was going to try a sweep and knock me off my feet. Deciding to take the hit, I dropped down into what we called a "horse stance," making myself as stable as possible.

    In a heartbeat he was on me, hitting my calf with his outstretched leg. The air was silent except for the sound of the river beside us and you could almost see the terror in his eyes as we made contact for the first time. He had the look of a man who had just kicked a deep-set telephone pole and his small body seemed lifeless as I grabbed him and sent him airborne with a modified hip throw.

Being accustomed to sparing with 200 pounders, I used a little too much force and all I could hear was Norma screaming "You're gonna kill him!" as I reached up and snatched him from the air, saving him from hitting the rocks along the river bank. We rolled from the sand, across the rocks into the icy cold water and laughed and sputtered as we clawed our way out of the current.

" Wow, did you see that" "that was awesome" (in Spanish, I think) or "Wow the fool nearly killed our guide!" I heard as the gang came to join us. Everyone except Norma wanted to spar and I told our guide that I was too tired to continue, leaving him to deal with it while Norma and I bathed in the river.

The water was shivering cold but nobody seemed to mind. Our host broke out a bottle of river-cooled rum and coke and we had a party on the beach after bathing. Chicken was roasting on sticks on the campfire and the cook was busy fixing mashed potatoes and onions. The meal was enhanced with wine and bottled water. Life was good.

After eating, we finished off the wine and visited. Two of the guests were from Spain and one from the Dominican Republic. None spoke much English but we were able to communicate quite well. Spanish lessons were paying off!

We found our way to freshly made beds in the room that resembled an old chicken coop back home. We brushed our teeth by candlelight, then collapsed in our bunks and fell quickly asleep. Norma was given her own sleeping quarters while the rest of us slept in an open bay in bunk beds, reminiscent of basic training camp.

Early the next morning, we were awakened to the smell of fresh coffee and something resembling a western omelet. With the falls still watching from above, we loaded our gear and sped away down stream in the canoe. The rapids, now somewhat familiar, took on a new personality as we were swept along quickly by the fast current. The trip back took only about two and a half hours.

Arriving back at the base camp, three of our companions quickly dressed and disappeared in the canoe, heading for home while Norma and I prepared for a quiet lunch and supper.

We had the camp to ourselves and after finishing a gourmet supper with some excellent wine, we watched as rain showers developed over the valley. This created a uniquely primitive atmosphere that made us feel as if we were the only two people in the world.

Thunder rumbled, lasting the longest time, with no lightning to be seen as we walked hand in hand in the darkness on the little trail leading towards our cabaña.

"Lets get showered up and pack most of our stuff tonight before they shut off the generator," Norma said as we entered our little cabin and turned on the light. We hugged and looked into each other's eyes and shared a kiss just as a loud rolling thunder began working its way across the valley. Little tingles of excitement rolled up and down my spine keeping in rhythm with the thunder and I could tell this was going to be a special night.

We set to work doing our chores as we talked about all of the events of this extraordinary jungle trip. There were two small bunk beds in our cabin and we turned down the sheets and inspected for scorpions and other varmints. As Norma climbed into the bunk across the room, I opened the door to peer out at the weather.

In the blink of an eye, a bright green eight-inch-long lizard scampered between my bare feet, headed straight for my turned down bunk, and disappeared!

Just then, the lights went out as the generator was shut down, leaving me blinded in the freshly created darkness. I quickly shut the door in case Mr. Lizard had a friend and staggered around the room in search of the flashlight that I had left near the head of my bunk.

Norma giggled safely from her bunk all the while making comments like " He wasn't very big, I don't think his bite will hurt much!" With the aid of my flashlight, I tore off the bedding in search of the vile looking creature but he was nowhere to be found.

"Maybe I should bunk with you tonight," I suggested with more than the lizard on my mind. "No you can't—there is barely room for me in here. I really don't think that it's the kind that bites and besides we know he can't possibly be in your bed."

"Damn it," I said under my breath as I again shook out the sheets, re-installed them on my bunk and climbed in. The gentle rain turned into the deafening roar of a full-blown rainstorm with lighting flashing in the windows and the floor shaking with each clap of thunder. I lay there for a while wondering if the river beside our cabaña would rise up and wash us and Mr. Lizard away into the darkness.

Norma was already snoring loudly and I don't think she even knew it was storming. Finally, my worries gave in to the exhaustion and I fell asleep.

By morning, the storm had ended; we had not washed away, and Mr. Lizard was nowhere to be found. The sun was shinning brightly and the pleasant aroma of breakfast being prepared permeated the camp.

After breakfast we finished packing, said our goodbyes while our luggage was loaded into the canoe, and soon we found ourselves being whisked away down stream in the strong current towards home.

In no time, our plane landed on the tiny runway near where we were waiting and its pilot climbed out and started unloading cargo boxes. I went over and gave him a hand, and soon all of the boxes were neatly stacked along the runway.

We took off in the calmness of the fresh jungle air, circled the beautiful river, and then headed back towards civilization.

The pilot remembered that I had flown a Cessna 150 from a previous conversation, and since there were only the three of us, asked if I would like to take the controls. The plane had only one yoke and he turned it over to me as he offered a few instructions, then climbed in the back to visit with Norma. She had never flown with me before and now it was her turn to worry.

What a thrill flying over the jungle, rivers, and falls! This was in stark contrast to seeing the wheat, corn, and bean fields back home and my mind's eye will re-live this event for years to come.

The GPS kept us on course in the sky just like the one on *Happy Ours* guides us thru the ocean and all too soon, the Orinoco

River crept into sight; it was time once again to become just a passenger as I relinquished the controls and prepared for a landing.

Another enjoyable trip in Venezuela was to a town called Merida with Bob, Marta and their beautiful daughter. Marta was the one that taught us some Spanish while we were in Trinidad so for sure there would be no language problems—right? Wrong, first thing on the bus at the airport, I was proudly speaking to Marta in my newly acquired language when everyone on the bus broke out in laughter. I had announced to the world that we were going to mierda (shit) instead of Merida and the locals thought it was very funny.

We flew in to Caracas, changed planes, then off to Merida. Good luck from the start—the sky was clear and the plane flew just off the coast, retracing the path we had sailed coming back from Bonaire. It was fun recognizing some of the landmarks from the sky. Turning left, we flew between two mountain ranges; Andes on one side and the Sierra Nevada's on the other. The view was awesome. Normally there are too many clouds and the plane flies over cloudy lake Maracaibo instead but not that day, the weather was perfect.

Merida is a college town in the mountains, which reminded us of Boulder, Colorado with lots of mountain bikes, pizza, and, young people. We spent only three nights in town, as it was noisy and crowded. There was an ice cream store there that boasted having more flavors than any other store in the country and as penalty for loosing a bet, I had agreed to eat what ever flavor my friends selected—How bad can that be?

Nearly gagging, I spooned down my first taste of trout ice cream, which had been carefully prepared by squeezing the oil from the limp body of a freshly caught trout. Norma and our friends watched with glee, as they made sure I swallowed the nasty, smelly concoction. No one even wanted a taste!

One night was spent in a hotel resembling a castle in the mountains (five star), and a couple of nights in a remolded plantation in one of the valleys. I was careful to secure lodging with no ice cream stores near. Christmas decorations were still up and everywhere we went the color and spirit of the Holidays still existed.

Several field trips introduced us to coffee plantations, sugar cane farming, power tourist shopping, and all of it with the beautiful mountains looming around us. We hiked up a mountain trail to view giant condors, another peak led us to a Catholic shrine, yet another to view only clouds, much like what happened to us on our visit to Pikes Peak in the U.S. The mountains are doted with small villages, each having a square, a large Catholic Church, many shops, and a few questionable restaurants. History here dates back to the 16th century when the Spaniards came in the search for gold. They found none.

Upon our return from Merida, we learned of a wine tasting party that was going to be held at Madrigal Village, a two-day sail from the marina. Sponsored by the Venezuelan vintners, it was to be an all night party with Steak dinners, various cheeses and hors d'oeuvres, unlimited beer, wine and live entertainment all for twenty-five dollars U.S.

Charlie Alpha arranged ground transportation and lodging for those who didn't want to go by boat. We chose boat as there were several things to do up in the Gulf of Cariaco and we had never been there before. We planned for at least ten days of exploring and partying. It was necessary to stay out of the water this trip mostly because of the number of large jellyfish, the largest we've ever seen; basketball size with streamers about a foot long. Jellyfish weren't the only large things on this trip. Dolphins swam on either side of *Happy Ours* spouting water much like whales do. They were gigantic and fascinating to watch.

Traveling with three other yachts for safety, we spent the first night anchored in Mochima National park, a beautiful collection of colorful mountain tops protruding from the water, and a cute little town called Mochima.

The second night, we anchored in a place called Laguna Grande on the northern side of the gulf. Here the beautiful surrounding mountains with their vivid colors left us in awe as we sat and watched the golden light of sunset play upon them.

A couple of nights later found us at Medregal Village, a little bit of paradise all its own. This grass hut bar, restaurant and hotel offered beautiful sunset views during happy our and dinner. There were many yachts anchored here; some had been there for months.

As luck would have it, the only direction the anchorage is exposed to foul weather, hosted a terrific storm the night we arrived. Many boats drug their anchors and one even had its bow pulpit ripped off in the violent waves. No one dared leave their boats unattended and we all spent a nervous night aboard. On the following day, we were greeted with calm winds and bright sunshine and dinked ashore to enjoy the beginnings of an awesome party.

At five p.m. the first beer and wine was served ceremonially with special snacks and the party began in earnest. We ate, drank, and, danced until the early hours of the morning. Not knowing the cruisers appetite for wine, the last of the red was gone by 2am. As we walked down to the dingy dock, we laughed at the sights we saw. The place was covered with people asleep, lying in chairs and some were even on the ground. Charley Alpha and his wife were curled up in separate lounge chairs, snoring away. The food had been delicious and so was the wine—a time we'll never forget although the price we paid the next morning for having so much fun was formidable.

On the far western shore of the Gulf is a sleepy fishing village called Muelle De Cariaco. It's sleepy because the fishermen must have stayed up all night either fishing or partying. It was Carnival time and loud entertainment boomed *out* over the water night and day.

Everyone was happy and helpful. We dinked ashore and were greeted by the smiling ash decorated faces of children anxious to help us secure our lines. They followed us thru town to the various little shops as if one of us were the pied piper himself. Of course, we found enough candy and gum in one of the shops to cement the bonds of friendship.

The next morning we loaded the dinks with sun lotion, cameras, drinks and snacks and proceed up the small river that empties into the gulf. It quickly narrowed to a mangrove covered stream winding its way through the countryside. Jungle sounds surrounded us and everywhere we looked offered a new exotic but primitive panorama. Several times we lifted the motors and paddled our way against the current. Stumps and snags were common and navigation was both fun and frightening.

The elusive red ibis stopped and posed for photographs along the way; we were told they are bright red from eating the plentiful shrimp in this area. Strange birds flew by as we dinked along, most of which we couldn't find in our bird books.

Our wakes sent shivers thru the water causing an eerie creaking sound from the tree roots as we carefully ghosted along. We finally came to a place where a large tree had fallen across the water and the only way to pass would have been to carry the heavy dink around and over it. This ended our trek. The next several hours found us drifting along with the current, listening to the strange sounds and drinking up the beautiful sights offered by this secluded place.

Our final day was spent on tour with Jean Mark back at the village. He took us by van to some caves that housed thousands of guacharo birds. These bat like creatures come out only late evening to feed and spend their days resting in caves. They are known as oilbirds because of the black oily looking mess they leave on the cave floor from their droppings. Pity the few of us that wandered around in the dark with open toed shoes!

We followed a guide with an oil lantern along a dark winding path in the cave, listening to the pre-historic sounds emanating from the darkness that surrounded us. Occasionally, a flicker of light from the lantern illuminated small mouse like critters that sat on the rocks and watched us pass. The whole thing was spooky and dark. No flashlights were allowed for fear of disturbing the inhabitants of the cave. A washing station was provided at the end of the tour where we could clean off the "oil" and was a welcome sight to most of us.

Our trip back to Puerto La Cruz was pleasant and un-eventful, wind was too light to sail and seas were flat and calm. Friends and dock mates greeted us with smiles and a welcome back party.

We took advantage of the cheap airfare and Joined Pat and Tom on *Ishmael* for a trip to Peru and Bolivia and what an experience! We saw strange creatures up in the mountains - a rabbit with a squirrel's tail, llamas, alpacas, giant condors, and an assortment of bugs and butterflies. Our first dung beetle was a perfect showman and rolled llama's do do along a trail for our entertainment.

The air was thin at altitudes of about 5000 meters and coming from sea level took its toll on all of us. Cocoa tea and candy helped, it is illegal to take this stuff out of the country but it really was a key to survival on this vacation.

First we flew to Lima, spent the night, and then grabbed a bus to Nazka. Here we chartered a small plane and flew over the famous ancient drawings that can only be seen from the air. The sky was clear and we had calm winds to make this a successful picture taking opportunity. We could clearly see the monkey, hummingbird, spider, and the spaceman as well as others as we circled over this desolate place.

That afternoon, we went to a one thousand year old cemetery. It was out in the desert all by itself and the grounds were strewn with bones and clothe used to wrap the mummies. A thousand years of grave robbers have taken its toll. The state now guards these graves night and day and there are a few tombs, which have been opened for display.

The dead were interred in a setting position with their knees bent up under their chin. One in particular was fascinating; he had been a shaman with extremely long hair, which had been draped carefully over posts that protruded from the walls of the tomb. He was setting there with his skull slightly tilted up, as if to greet us with his sinister, toothy grin. I can still close my eyes and see him today.

An overnight bus ride took us to Arequipa where we enjoyed a city tour and the following day found us on an all day tour of Colca Canyon where we watched giant Condors soar on the air currents created by the mountains.

There were no guardrails on the lookout areas and we soon learned to take responsibility for our own safety. Our van broke down and we were directed to start down the mountain on foot, as it was getting late in the day. The guide went with us, leaving the driver alone to make the repairs. There was a narrow, winding trail that we followed on the way down and the scenery made the walk worth it. Cactus towered above us and the beautiful valley below came into view, providing a bird's eye look at the lush green farmland on either side of the winding river. Just before dark we heard the sound of our van as it came to a screeching stop on the road adjacent to the trail. It was setting lopsided but seemed to be running ok. A rear suspension spring had broken on the way up and the driver used rope to tie what was left of the spring to the axle in order for us to get out of there before dark. Bumps and thumps kept us on the edge of our seats but we made it back to the hotel in one piece.

We boarded an airplane and flew to Cuzco the next morning. This is a great tourist town with lots of museums, cathedrals, and ancient ruins. When the Spaniards forced the Catholic religion upon the Indians, they didn't openly resist—The Virgin Mary became the earth goddess, etc. The only clues that the old ways still exist are in the paintings and music. One cathedral had a painting of the last supper with all of the local dishes on the table including guinea pig, a favorite. Another picture depicted the conquistadors crucifying Jesus instead of the Romans. It is a mixed up world.

From Cuzco, we took a train to Machupicchu where we spent two days exploring the lost city. As the train switched back and forth up the mountain in a zigzag pattern, we looked nervously at the twisted steel rail that littered the mountainside—remnants of a recent mudslide. We arrived about three p.m. and were quickly ushered onto buses, which took us to the lost city high above. We enjoyed the guided tour but were a little put off by the tremendous crowd. People were everywhere, making picture taking difficult as our guide herded us from place to place.

Instead of taking the train back that evening, we secured lodging in a small town at the base of the mountain for the night. After enjoying a quick breakfast, we boarded a bus and headed back up the mountain without a guide. The place was nearly deserted and its magic came to life. Having taken pictures to our heart's content, we climbed up to the gate and even followed the difficult trail back to a ruin on the mountainside.

We met a group that had been on the trail for several days coming from the opposite direction and were glad that we hadn't talked ourselves into that arduous trip. Their feet were blistered, they were cold, tired, exhausted and all were much younger than us.

The climb up the mountain trail to the gate was made difficult by the thin air, but was well worth it; To view the city from the far away gate was a real thrill. This is the same gate thru which the sun's rays illuminate an altar in the city below during the solstice. It also offered the first view that visiting priest had of the magnificent city after making their long journey along the difficult mountain trails.

On the way down, the others went on while I took time out to meditate and repair a small stone monument to Patchamama, placing it among those built by the old priest centuries ago.

Having visited nearly every ruin back in Cuzco, we headed to Puno on lake Titikaka. From there we visited the floating islands, made totally from reeds and then took a bus to the southern part of the lake to a town called Copacabana in Bolivia.

Chartering a private boat, we visited ruins on the islands of the sun and moon, where we explored a stone labyrinth atop of the island of the sun, near the sacred rock. We were told God, when he first set foot on Earth, made a strange gigantic footprint that is preserved in the rock of the trail leading to the top. It was so big, it was easy to spot and unlike anything we had seen before.

The following day we went back to the mainland and finished our trip with a look at the Tiwinaku ruins near La Paz. Here we found a magnificent temple, surrounded by giant stone sculptures carved with symbols of the past. Excavation has halted because of lack of funding and a great deal of this magnificent place remains hidden; buried by the centuries. Many of the structures had been torn down and the stones used to erect a nearby Catholic Church.

English wasn't widely used and we had no reservations past the first night; however, twenty-one days later we made it safely back to *Happy Ours*. The <u>Lonely Planet</u> had been a very useful resource and I would recommend it.

We flew home for a visit, returned to have *Happy Ours* hauled for bottom paint, then provisioned up to leave beautiful Venezuela.

Chapter 13

Life After Venezuela

Blanquilla, a beautiful island with white sand beaches just one hundred nm north of Puerto La Cruz was our first destination. It is isolated and provides and overnight anchorage for fisherman. There are a few military men stationed there, other than that, occasionally a cruiser will visit this out of the way place. Shelling on the beach was wonderful and Norma collected a tub full of almost perfect specimens—one of her favorite pastimes.

We anchored near a couple of old fishing boats in a little protected cove and were soon visited by the military. We shared some Coke and cold water as they inspected our paperwork. We were told that we could stay for as long as we needed and they headed over to check one of the fishing boats.

When climbing onboard, one of the men accidentally knocked the antenna off of their portable 2-way radio and it sank in about thirty feet of water. Wild with fear of military reprisal, they motored back to us and ask if we could loan them snorkel equipment. One of them was a diver, so I also loaned him a spare air to give him more bottom time to find the antenna. All went well and smiling faces returned our equip.ment. The following day, the fishing boat came along side and handed us a really nice fish for supper, compliments of the military.

When fueling up our dink to make the trip over to Americano Bay, we noticed one of the plastic gas cans on deck had ruptured, losing all of the precious contents overboard, and had gone unnoticed until then. We immediately contacted Geoffrey and Nancy on *Panache* and asked them to bring another container with gas when they joined us in a few days. They did and we were very grateful.

Americano Bay is a beautiful, secluded place on Blanquilla, getting its name from an American who settled there long ago. The ruins of his house are still there and a pristine white sand beach offers irresistible exploring opportunities.

Geoffrey, Nancy, and their wonder dog Charlie shared this beautiful place with us for nearly an entire day. Charlie and I dug holes in the sand and waited for a wave to fill them up, then Charley would jump in and splash around, barking wildly. If the holes had been larger, I might have joined him!

After having several days of fun, it was time to leave. *Panache* headed back to Puerto La Cruz and *Happy Ours* set sail west towards Los Roquies. The 130 km sail took us seventeen hours and we arrived as planned just after dawn. We found a beautiful, populated island with its only one mountain towering above the surrounding ocean. The following day found us climbing that mountain to explore an ancient lighthouse that adorned the top. The view was breathtaking and so was the climb. Returning to the little village at the bottom, we purchased some potatoes, onions, and fresh bread and enjoyed a feast on *Happy Ours* that evening.

A fuel boat arrived the next day so we loaded the jerry cans in the dink and shagged fuel back and fourth until our tanks could hold no more.

We were soon joined by our old friends Carl and Mary Lou on *Starlight Dancer*, Wayne and Bibbie on *Discovery*, Roger and Frankie on *Infinity*, Rick and Robin on *Endangered Species*, John and Susan on *Zee Lander* and others.

We were all headed for Bonaire and decided to loosely travel together. All of us marveled at the sight of the Red footed booby birds nesting in the Avies and enjoyed the wonderful spear fishing everywhere. Food was plentiful; the water was warm and clear so we were in no hurry to leave these beautiful islands.

Wayne and Bibbie discovered a little place where there were hundreds of fan shells and we all spent the afternoon diving down and harvesting the delicious creatures. The rest of our time was spent cleaning and cooking. It was a feast to remember with everyone brining a dish to supplement the day's harvest.

Occasionally, we would gather on one of the boats for Dominos or cards and maybe to just enjoy a sundowner. The weather held and we eventually, one by one, set sail for Bonaire—a paradise all it's own.

Many of us were certified divers and purchased tank fills in bulk at a very reduced rate. We attended classes provided by the local dive shops on fish identification and once again, enjoyed each other's company, diving, drinking and partying in the various restaurants and pubs.

Soon, it was on to Curacou in the ABC's. We met up with even more friends: Bill and Nancy on *Cabaret*. Bill is an interesting fellow. He built his huge Catamaran himself and she was seaworthy as she was pretty. He was literally an expert on women having put himself thru medical school (specializing in Gynecology) as a hairdresser. Nancy said he was a great husband!

We needed to go home for a visit and Left *Happy Ours* in the safe hands of the owners of Keemakelkey Marina and flew to Kansas City.

Upon our return, we visited the various attractions of this colorful place, made some repairs, and set out for Cartagena. There was much discussion about whether to travel along the coast in groups, under motor or to stay well off the Colombian coast and sail. Pirates were known to be active in the small bays along the coast and sometimes ignored the fact there was more than one yacht. On the other hand, the ocean passage was said to be the fifth most difficult in the world because wind and steep waves would quickly build in this area.

Starlight Dancer had already left for Aruba and reported having had a nice sail. We found what looked like a good weather window and headed out alone, opting to sail instead of motor. Sail! The conditions were perfect, so good in fact that we found ourselves off the coast of Aruba in the middle of the night.

A young tourist girl named Natalie Holloway from the U.S. was missing from her hotel in Aruba and foul play was suspected.

Officials were searching the coastline for her and this, coupled with the nasty, degrading comments we had heard from some of the locals, caused us to take advantage of the excellent sailing and convinced us to just keep heading west.

For two nights and three days, we enjoyed an absolutely perfect down-wind sail. Taking turns on watch allowed us both time to read and relax. *Happy Ours* scooted along, swaying gently as she quickly gobbled up the miles towards Cartagena.

On the third night, things turned ugly and with the rapidly increasing wind came huge, rolling waves that would lift our stern high in the air as they passed us by. We broke out the inflatable life vest/harnesses and tethered ourselves to a secure cleat in the cockpit, then shortened sail by rolling in the jib and most of the main sail, all the while thanking God that all of this could be accomplished without leaving the safety of the cockpit.

Altering course to allow the wind Angel to fill the sails more from one side helped us to prevent a dangerous jibe from occurring; however doing so took us further from our destination. I rigged a preventer to keep the boom in place just incase the wave action was stronger than the wind in hopes that we wouldn't break anything. The Single Sideband radio net had reported serious flooding on the mainland and trees and debris were reported to be flowing out into the ocean from the swollen rivers along the coast, creating a hazard to navigation. Being farther away from the coast on a pitch-black night did have its advantages.

Wind up to forty-five knots was consistently being displayed on our instruments with an occasional ninety-nine knots reading, when the tip of the mast swung violently as *Happy Ours* was heaved around in the towering seas. It only took a couple hours of this treatment before the sending unit broke and abruptly displayed all zeros.

Next to go was the preventer we had rigged on the main boom to keep it from swinging wildly in the wind and waves. I was able to reach thru a port and re-secure it without taking too much water in while the port was open.

We zipped down the cockpit enclosures, and tried to keep a sharp lookout while the faithful autopilot fought to maintain course.

Having the plastic windows zipped and snapped down gave us warmth, and the false sense of security that accompanies it. Still tethered, Norma stretched out in the cockpit, tied herself to a winch to keep from rolling off her cushion, and quickly fell asleep.

After about an hour, I took off my harness and laid it on a cushion to go below to answer nature's call. Many a sailor has been lost at sea by trying to relieve themselves over the side and I had no intention of becoming one of those statistics.

The cabin was a mess with books, charts, clothing, and cooking utensils flying about and I didn't dare to turn on the lights and destroy my night vision. Stubbing my toe on unidentified objects along the way, I found finally the aft head. Just when I was ready, a rogue wave smashed into our side, laying *Happy Ours* on her beam-ends. With her deep full keel, she quickly recovered but by then I was no longer in the head but somewhere in the galley with my pants unzipped. I had just made my way back when I heard Norma screaming my name, her voice barely discernable over the wind and the sledge hammering sound of the waves smashing against the hull.

When the wave hit us, it ripped the windows open, inundating Norma and the cockpit with salt water. The cockpit was full and the scuppers were barely able to keep up. Having been awakened from a sound sleep so abruptly, Norma looked around and couldn't find me. Fearing the worst, she started staring out to sea in search of her favorite captain who must have been washed overboard.

I detected real fear in her voice and decided she needed me more than I needed to go to the bathroom and headed for the companionway to re-assure her I was ok. She was soaking wet and the cockpit drains were still running full blast. I told her I was going to finish my business and headed back down below,

Just before I was ready to return to duty, I heard a louder "Bob-Bob there is something up here! It is swimming around in the cockpit and it's trying to get me." I raced up the stairs to take a look and found Norma cowering with her knees drawn up under her chin. Sure enough, there was something swimming around up there. Grabbing a small flashlight, I took a better look.

Our sea monster turned out to be my life vest, which inflated automatically when the big wave came aboard. It seemed to have a life of it's own as the harness strap became a long tail swimming furiously behind it's bulky body. A horrible battle ensued and I finally dispatched the creature and slung it below. I checked our course, found some dry clothing for both of us, put on the spare harness and clipped it to the safety ring.

We zipped the windows and snapped them back into place as the last of the water drained out of the cockpit. Luckily no water found its way below and the waves had stopped flooding in so things were getting back to normal at last.

I mentioned being a little hungry and a wet; nasty pillow came flying at my head. I took that as a no! Coca Cola has enough sugar and caffeine to help us thru a night watch so that, with a hand full of mixed nuts had to suffice.

At last, dawn started illuminating our surroundings, first with a pale yellow hew, giving way to the brighter light of early morning. We were astonished to see the size of the surrounding waves—they had nearly doubled in size from the previous evening, dwarfing our little 44-foot sailboat. White foam crests were breaking everywhere and the towering waves alternately concealed the horizon, and then set us seemingly on top of the world. We were alone; had not seen another vessel for the past two days, and there was no land in sight.

"This is another fine freaking mess you have gotten us into." Norma shouted to me as she headed below to figure out how to brew some coffee. "No, you couldn't just motor along the coast with our friends like normal people—you had to be macho and prove something by sailing all the way! You'll not do this to me again!" she shouted as she had her first glance at the mess below.

She found by turning on the inverter and putting the coffee pot in the sink so it wouldn't turn over, we could safely perk this precious liquid. We enjoyed a couple of cups each and hungrily woofed down some breakfast bars to help us start our day.

We had purposely sailed past the waypoint on which we planned to turn south, fearing the prospect of taking the seas on our beam and maybe even rolling over in the night. Slowly we changed course and experimented with the way *Happy Ours* would respond in these extreme conditions, knowing that the seas would be calmer once we were sheltered by the tip of Columbia. A strong counter current and adverse wind hampered our progress but finally things got calmer and we were able to fire up the motor.

Unfortunately, when I tried to roll in the rest of the jib, a broken piece of bungi cord found it's way into the furler and jammed. Try as we would, the sail would neither roll out nor in. While we wrestled with that problem, one of our stopper knots came loose, allowing a jib sheet to pass thru its block and whip freely in the wind. The sail flapped hard enough and long enough that the protective UV cover tore loose and was in shreds. It's heavy metal clew with the accompanying jib sheets flopped violently out of control, lashing out at everything on deck. The only option to fix the problem was to stay clear of the clew by crawling on deck and clearing the drum. Taking off my inflatable life vest, I eased out of the cockpit and scooted on my back towards the bow of our boat, hanging on to the lifeline and jack line. A couple of times, the heavy rope that made up the jib sheet smacked me across the chest, leaving raised red whelps. As I approached the bow, it became necessary to time the waves and hold my breath when *Happy Ours'* bow and I disappeared rythmetically under the surface. Finally, I cleared the jam and as Norma effortlessly rolled in the jib, I re-rigged the jib sheet and made my way to the safety of the cockpit.

It took nearly all day to make good the forty nm to the small boat entrance of Cartagena and it soon became evident that it would be dark before arriving.

We decided to heave to, enjoy a nice warm supper of microwaved hamburger helper and a long awaited glass of wine. Taking turns standing watch during the night was a breeze in the calmer seas and we both got some well-deserved sleep.

The following morning after enjoying a leisurely breakfast, we double checked our position, installed a new course in the GPS, and motored in calm seas towards the entrance to the walled city. Red and green buoys clearly marked the place over which we could safely pass through a cut in the underwater wall that used to block the entrance. Peacefully we motored along, taking time to enjoy the beautiful statue setting on an island in the middle of the entrance.

An ancient old fort dominated the skyline on one side in stark contrast to the modern skyscrapers on the other. We motored over to an anchorage marked on our charts and wound in and around the many yachts occupying this space.

Finding a clear spot to anchor, we circled, checking the depths before deploying our ground tackle, all the while, returning the warm welcoming waves from cruisers we had yet to meet.

We showered, ate lunch and tidied up the boat. Next I launched the dink, installed the outboard motor and headed over to visit with a nearby cruiser. He told us where to dock and who best to contact for checking in, then invited us to join them for a party in Club Nautico Marina that evening.

Checking in was easy, there was an agent waiting for us at the marina dock who handled everything for a small fee. We visited with John, the friendly dock master and found there was an up-coming space available in the marina. Having agreed on a price, it was just a matter of time before enjoying air conditioning and other amenities.

We went wild at the party that night, making new friends and having lots of fun. It turned out that Club Nautico was the hub of cruiser activity in Cartagena and the bar/restaurant was home to most of the social activities—our kind of place!

Checking in at the marina office, we noticed a painting of a fellow cruiser we had enjoyed knowing in Venezuela hanging on the wall. When we pointed to the picture, excitedly calling out his name (Storman Norman), we were greeted with an uneasy frown and were immediately escorted to a back room where we were instructed that we had never seen this man.

It turned out that Norman was the husband of Canderliera, the owner of the marina and had escaped the country after having been falsely accused of drug trafficking. He was still wanted and the statue of limitations would soon expire. We admitted that we were mistaken—couldn't have been the same man and smiles returned.

We moved *Happy Ours* into the marina in a few days and began assessing the damage incurred during our stormy passage.

We learned what we had thought to be ten to twelve foot seas really had averaged eighteen to twenty. God only knows the size of the rogue wave that knocked us around in the middle of the night!

We discovered our old factory rigging with oversized stainless steel wire had been stressed to the point that fishhooks had developed in the shrouds and needed replaced. The rope that was used to hold the main sail out was reduced down to just a few remaining strands and one of the halyards was worn half in two. We had just about pushed *Happy Ours* to her limits! We replaced what we could there but the standing rigging was out of the question and would need to be replaced in Panama. The only thing left to do was enjoy!

Cruising friends from the past trickled in one by one and like us, discovered new friends in this wonderful city. The parties were fantastic and the marina proved to be a great home base, although we never were as close to the owners as we had been in Puerto La Cruz, Venezuela.

Walls surrounded the old city with the only entrance being an arched doorway under the old clock tower. We were told over a million slaves had been sold in the square and much gold had been exchanged. Today, up scale shops and restaurants line the streets and the specialty is emerald jewelry. I believe every boat sailed away with something green glistening in the sun.

There were many skilled street hustlers selling everything from t-shirts to hats and it was a big thing for them to lure you into a shop or restaurant. Once you made a purchase, the price seemed a little higher than it would have been had you gone in on your own. In some cases, we found it better to just say that we were not with them as we walked in the doorway.

The other side of the bay offered a beautiful white sand beach lined by expensive hotels and condos. Thousands of tourists competed for tables at the restaurants and bars and it felt as if we were back in Florida. Walking around the town, even at night proved relatively safe and we quickly learned the areas to avoid.

While there, I had a problem with an ATM giving me a receipt but no cash. When asking what to do, I was directed to a stocky rough looking character wearing a black eye patch named Hernando. He spoke some English and directed me to join him in a cab. We went to the old city, got out, and I was amused to see the amount of respect this fellow commanded from all the street people.

I followed him into one of the really big banks and wound up in an executive's office. Spanish was exchanged back and fourth much too quickly for me to understand and after some hand waving, I was told to contact our credit card company and a credit would appear on our account immediately.

I paid Hernando a small fee and we laughed and visited during the cab ride back to the marina.

I mentioned to Hernando that we needed to see some of the country and sure enough, he reached into his pocket and pulled out a laminated tourist guide card, clipped it on to his shirt and with a big grin asked how many wanted to go and where.

It didn't take long to fill up a mini bus with fellow cruisers. We had negotiated a reasonable discounted price and agreed to his itinerary only with the understanding that he furnish all the rum and cola we could drink. He lived up to his part of the bargain and we enjoyed cold rum and colas as we visited the old fort, parts of the walled city, his friend's jewelry shop, and a very interesting alligator farm. We stopped at a non-touristy restaurant and enjoyed a delicious meal along the way and were certainly tired and ready to return to the marina that afternoon.

Word was out about how much fun we had and the next Hernando special required a much larger bus. With forty-seven people on board, we headed north to visit the town of Santa Marta, the oldest city in Columbia. There is a beautiful old farm and museum there that was the place where Simon Bolivar died. People in South America get excited just hearing his name and the monument there reflects this.

Hernando took us to a strange and gory looking art exhibit displaying the works of Botero who painted pictures about the death and suffering of the Columbian people. He seemed to love to paint fat people, especially with bullet holes in them.

We visited several beautiful costal cities, but found the most interesting part was the trip itself. Of course Hernando furnished plenty of rum and colas and provided lively conversation, but there was more! Travel by bus in Columbia provided us with a panorama of deserted seashore, jungle, mountains and, really poor fishing villages that were surrounded by old wooden fishing boats with large square sails. Strange little market places stood along the highway where we stopped to sample some of the local cuisine and stretch our legs. Toilets were flushed with a furnished bucket of water and I never saw anything made out of paper in the rest rooms.

The main highways were in good repair. To remind us we weren't in the U.S., there were checkpoints with armed soldiers looking for guerillas. The sun reflected on bright shiny razor wire bordering the highway in some places where the Sierra Nevada Mountains terminated near the road. We were told it was not safe to travel by road at certain times, especially for gringos, but Hernando took care of things ahead of time and all was well.

It was a very long day trip and every so often, the bus would stop at a military looking checkpoint and only Hernando would get out. I watched him reach for his wallet more than once and disappear behind the guard shack with one of the uniformed men. I guess this was necessary to guarantee a smooth, safe passage. All he ever would tell me was that we shouldn't attempt to travel up there on our own—especially at night.

Hernando could do other things as well. He found a cheap supplier for shrimp and would bring them to our boat in black trash bags for pickup by the other cruisers. He always gave us an honest measure and was a good friend.

Around Christmas time, Cartagena came alive with brightly colored Christmas lights and decorations. We took a tour in an open-air party bus and enjoyed seeing the place in its Holiday splendor.

Early in January 2006, we flew to Medellin with the crew of *Gonzo2*. This is a city in the Colombian mountains noted for its beauty and it's wonderful display of Christmas lights. Medellin is in a valley between the mountains and has a river running its full length. Along side the river, they have developed a train system that can quickly take you to any part of the city for a small sum. It terminates on one end at a sky lift, which takes you several levels up the mountain to various suburbs. It was not designed for tourists but is great fun to ride.

The Christmas lights are all over the city but are especially concentrated along the river, where professionals hoping to sell their work on the worldwide market exhibited the displays. Other attractions were a beautiful castle furnished with expensive antiques, several museums, statues sculpted by Boltero, beautiful old churches, good restaurants, and giant shopping malls.

We took an eight-hour driving tour through several villages and over the mountains in order to view a large meteor that is said to be 2/3rds under ground. To our surprise they have installed a system of 700 stairs so tourist can climb to the top and enjoy the view.

It overlooks a series of lakes with little mountain top islands peeping out from the water below. At the end of these lakes is a bridge that has military guards blocking it. Our guide told us that on the other side of this bridge there were still guerillas. It was explained to us that all of this area was controlled by the drug lords as recently as two years ago and has been re-claimed a little at a time.

They view their country as being at war with these drug people and they expect to win it all back in the next couple of years. Our guide had even purchased property on the other side of this bridge without having ever seen it. He hopes that its value will increase greatly when the war is over. We didn't invest; however, it was tempting.

Our original tour package included a tour of the lights, three night's lodging and transportation to and from the airport and hotel. They tried to make us pay extra to go on the lights tour bus but we refused, opting to take the matter up with the hotel manager. The following night we boarded the bus with no additional charge and enjoyed seeing all of the lights. This helped prepare us for the next attempted rip off.

Upon checkout from the hotel, we requested the clerk to arrange for our free transportation to the airport. In a few minutes, a car arrived and we were told our transportation was there. I verified with the front desk that this was indeed our driver and was told yes. Showing the driver our vouchers he nodded in acceptance; however, upon our arrival at the airport he demanded fifty dollars U.S. We all gave him the vouchers and refused to pay another nickel. We walked quickly to the luggage check and were tagging our bags when we looked up to see the cabbie with some armed military types heading our way—this was not good!

They ushered us into the airline office where there was an interpreter and the fun began. The more the driver waved his arms and pointed, the louder we became as we waved the vouchers at him. We demanded to speak with the hotel manager, which the lady at the front desk avoided at all cost when the airline called for us. The young military man in charge called his Commandant, who showed up and angrily demanded we pay the driver or we wouldn't be allowed to leave. Bud and Judy, being stubborn cruisers like ourselves, gave no quarter. We all sat down and folded our arms in unison, still demanding that the hotel manager be contacted.

Dismayed with our noisy display in the airport (a crowd was starting to gather) the Commandant insisted to speak with the manager. When the manager answered, the phone was given to the driver who was instructed to collect the vouchers and return to the hotel for payment—a lot less than fifty dollars U.S. We were allowed to board the plane and waved good by to our newfound military friends who, after the Commandant left, were smiling and friendly.

There are lots of stories from Cartagena that must be left untold for now because of space; however I can tell you we all had fun and loved it there.

Several boats rendezvoused at an anchorage just west of Cartagena in a group of islands called The Rosarios. In addition to some nice restaurants were a bird sanctuary and an aquarium type place called the Oceanario. It took only a couple of days to see all that was available and it was time to move on. David and Terry on Sylvester and a British couple on a trimaran left with us from there for an overnight sail to the beautiful San Blas Islands, while other yachts opted to follow along the coast or wait for more calm weather.

Chapter 14

Panama

Our companion boats disappeared in regular intervals as we all slipped up and over the wave crests. Most of the 180 km trip was in rough seas and twenty-knot winds. We arrived just after dawn and found our way to a popular anchorage called the Swimming Hole.

After enjoying a good night's sleep, we moved on to check in at Isla Porvenir, and then felt free to explore all of the island chain. The islands were small, mostly covered with palm trees and surrounded by white sand beaches with crystal clear water. Most of them were uninhabited except for a few Kuna fishermen that found shelter during the night under makeshift structures made from palm leaves.

Sylvester hung with us and together we explored about ten islands and three villages at a very leisurely pace. Many an afternoon would find us playing cards or dominos after spending the day exploring beautiful deserted islands, swimming and snorkeling in the refreshing clean water, and taking pictures until our fingers were tired.

Occasionally a Kuna supply boat would drop by and sell us vegetables, beer, wine, and soda. Kuna women would drift up in dugout canoes and offer to sell us molas(a needle work patch of art that they are known for) and the men always had fresh lobster, fish, crabs, and an occasional octopus for sale or trade.

Cruisers of all nationalities were enjoying that beautiful place and the laid back camaraderie with fellow sailors. Nearly all of us maintained watch on the VHF radio—not always good, as I'll explain.

The Kuna Indians are a vanishing breed that has maintained their culture no matter what. The women there are boss and are in charge of making molas to sell. Homosexuality is rampant and we understand the first born male is raised feminine if there are no girl children in the family. He is taught the art of mola making and is held in high regard in their society.

Unfortunately, the best-looking Kuna woman we found turned out to be a man. She showed up soon after we anchored with a couple of children in her canoe. Her name was Lisa and she had long dark hair and a beautiful complexion. When she finished showing us her molas, she headed over to *Sylvester* and on the VHF, I announced that he might consider buying something from this beautiful creature. When she left his boat, he called back, agreeing with me that she was beautiful—Big Mistake. Everyone for miles around overheard our conversation and most all of them already knew about Lisa. You could almost here the laughing in the anchorage with out the aid of the radio as one by one, the good-natured comments flooded in. All Dave and I could do was laugh with them, but she really was pretty.

Being on our own out there for months was an experience we'll probably never forget. Communication to family and friends was via sailmail on the SSB radio. My niece Julie, and kid brother EC notified us that my stepsister Cheryl wanted to purchase dad's old house and to settle dad's estate; we needed to have a document notarized. Sounds simple except for where we were.

We enlisted the aid of a fellow that came to us in a dugout canoe. He made an appointment with the Secretary of the Chief of the Kunas at the island of Nargana. At the appointed time, we met at the secretary's home, which was a hut, made from bamboo and covered with a thatch type roof. He witnessed our signatures and two days later we had paperwork with the official seal of the Kuna Nation, Island of Nargana; five dollars for the guy in the canoe, five dollars for the secretary, and three dollars to have the post office opened on a holiday and to send the letter. It arrived intact about fourteen days later.

That chore behind us, we took on some fuel and water and sailed on. We were about eighty miles from the Panama Canal and really needed to make some repairs. Our friend Tom on *Meema* had helped us keep the freezer limping along, but it was using way too much energy for our batteries. The water maker cat pump had given up the ghost and even the generator was acting up. Our rigging still had fishhooks in the shrouds and it was definitely time to go. There is just so much of beautiful white sand, palm trees, lobster and crab that we could stand.

Sailing along the coast of Panama was easy, we put in at Lintone, spent the night, then on to Puertobelo. Leaving *Happy Ours* and *Sylvester* safely at anchor in this protected harbor, we took a bus to Colon for a day trip to make arrangements for slips at the old Panama Canal Yacht Club.

Loud music was blasting from monstrous speakers on the bus and the driver was a mad man, but some how we made it. We found Colon to be not so nice of a place—tired, dirty, and dangerous. We quickly hailed a taxi and made our way to the yacht club. Once inside, we felt a little safer and were able to secure dockage for both boats. The bus ride back was a little better, knowing that our mission was accomplished.

In a few days, we sailed into our assigned slips at the yacht club, dodging large ships along the way. There were twenty-three ships anchored out side the breakwater waiting their turn to enter the harbor and it was fun to time our entrance around the green buoy, slipping in-between a tanker and a container ship. Once in, we found it safer to motor outside the channel markers where the big ships dared not go because of their deep draft. Every ship that passed thru the canal would use this same channel and it wasn't a good place to be in the way.

Panama Canal Yacht Club was located just off of the entrance to the Panama Canal. Our slip was out on the first marina dock, a location exposed to the wakes of passing ships, pilots, and tugs. The up side was watching the never-ending parade of different shipping, ranging from military war ships to the interesting looking container ships of various flags and the brightly lit cruise ships.

Adjacent to our slip was a busy shipyard where containers were unloaded and carefully stacked by giant cranes. The sound of containers being stacked, ships sounding signals with their deep throated horns, constant chatter on the VHF radio, welders and workmen banging and chattering away all made this an exciting place to be. Norfolk was quiet in comparison.

Seldom a minute went by that there wasn't something interesting to watch and Norma and I both could be caught yelling, "Honey, come look at this!" She was truly the perfect cruising companion.

It was hot and humid with tropical proportions and we were glad to have the air conditioning on.

Many of our friends came here and the same party-like atmosphere prevailed as in other marinas along the way. There was a bar and restaurant on the premises, and a taxi was always available to take us to town. Taking a taxi was a necessity as danger lurked just outside of the marina fence. Many cruisers were robbed during the short walk to town; eight unfortunate cruisers donated their money during our brief stay there.

The taxi drivers also served as agents to help us get checked in and all were well versed in how to get us in to the Free Zone to shop in this giant, duty free complex.

The marina had on staff some quality workers who could do everything from haul and paint your boat bottom to some light welding and mechanical repairs.

We found a fellow named Richard Brooker who was an excellent rigger and put him to work on re-rigging *Happy Ours*. To save money and to learn about rigging, I agreed to be his assistant. We immediately got started measuring the rig and inspecting turnbuckles, etc.

Richard decided all of the turnbuckles should be replaced and saved enough money to pay for them by using new factory rigging in lieu of stay-locks or other aftermarket devises, as I had planned to do originally.

He was very professional in doing the work and I learned that I never wanted to be a rigger. It is much more difficult than I had imagined. Having patience is a big part of the job—it took several months to get everything shipped to Panama before the work could begin.

While we were waiting, we enjoyed a tour of the canal, several trips to Panama City where we could find boat parts, water maker parts, and even St Louis style BBQ. Norma and the ladies enjoyed shopping at the very large shopping mall near the bus station as well as on the streets full of local venders.

Norma and I got a chance to work as line handlers on the boat *Pathfinder*, owned by some delightful Aussies, Hub, Rose, and their daughter Sara. We truly enjoyed an over-night transit of the canal.

A captain and 4 line handlers are required, providing an opportunity for some locals to gain extra income by helping out short-handed crews. Our deal was for meals, wine, and bus fare back to *Happy Ours*—a considerable savings for our newfound friends, as the going rate was all of that plus $150 US each.

The pilot boat dropped off our pilot about six P.M and we were soon underway for the first lock. Night passages are common for small boats as they are much cheaper.

The blackness of a cloudy, dark night quickly settled around us and we excitedly motored along in the darkness. All of a sudden, five blood-chilling blasts signaling danger emanated from a large ship behind us and nearly caused me to jump overboard. Our pilot quickly directed us to move out of the channel to safety and a monstrous mass of steel chugged by, late for its canal appointment.

We arrived, rafted up with a large powerboat, and proceeded into the first lock. Since the powerboat was so much larger than our forty-one foot sailboat, they drove, and handled all the lines. As the huge gates closed behind us, the lock quickly flooded with water, effortlessly elevating all that would float. As soon as we were elevated, the gate opened and we motored into the next lock, where the same thing occurred. When the gates opened on the third lock, we untied from the powerboat and headed out into the lake on our own.

About midnight we were in the lake between the two locks and our pilot directed us to tie up to a buoy for the night—the pilot left and we all celebrated. At six AM the next morning a new pilot was banging on the side of our boat wanting to get going. We were all still asleep, hung over and exhausted. Comical confusion ensued as we prepared to get under weigh.

After about a twenty-six nm journey across the lake, we tied to a dock and waited our turn to enter the final three locks. Our lake trip had been a short five hours of dodging ships, barges, tugs, dredges, and even an animal that looked like an alligator. The lake itself was beautiful and reminded us of Truman Lake back home, only bigger.

For the next three locks, we rafted to another sailboat and were directed to handle the lines on our side and the other vessel handled the lines on the other. The pilot excused the women from duty and explained if something went wrong he wanted as much beef as he could get on the lines. Nothing went wrong and we had become expert line handlers.

After clearing the third lock, we cast the lines loose from our raft-up and motored under the Bridge of Americas in search of the old famous Balboa Yacht club. We secured to a mooring ball and headed to shore via a provided motor launch for some much need refreshment. It seemed funny to us how the Pacific resembled the Atlantic in the Canal Zone.

Norma and I secured a hotel room for the night and spent the next day exploring beautiful Panama City. We shopped, met some friends for a visit, and then took a cab back to Colon where *Happy Ours* was birthed.

We were tired from the adventure and spent the day napping and relaxing. We took some great pictures of our transit and had a new story to tell.

We scheduled a haul out date at the yacht club for new bottom paint and wanted to try out our new rigging so we set sail back to the San Blas for another look at those beautiful islands. We now had a working water maker, new freshly tuned rigging, and plenty of fuel and supplies; however, our short stay was marred by a nasty storm that lasted three days.

Seeing the forecast, we took *Happy Ours* to a well-protected anchorage behind the town of Nargana. Other boats were there including *Patcha Mamma* and we were all assisted by our old friend in the dugout canoe who had helped us get a notary stamp previously. He helped us space apart so as to have plenty of swinging room for the upcoming storm and we all let out a ten to one scope.

The severity of the storm was as promised, with winds so strong *Happy Ours* more than once was laid over on her side, swinging wildly on her anchor. The rain catcher was torn to shreds and the 3/4" snubber that we rigged to reduce the shock load of chain rode, ripped in two. When it really got bad, I would sit in the cockpit, at the helm with our motor running in gear to relive some of the pressure on the anchor and to be ready in case it turned loose.

We learned that some of the Kuna huts were blown away and that a child was drowned. Some sailboats were sunk in Lintone and the dingy dock was torn apart. Back in Colon, two ships had drug and were on the rocks at the entrance to the canal and that many of our friends had drug at anchor with varying degrees of damage.

On our sail back to Colon, we witness what appeared to be the aftermath of a nautical battle. We had never seen enormous ships setting on the breakwater before and pondered our extreme good fortune during this ordeal.

The bottom paint job went smooth, delayed only by the repairs to a sailboat that had been holed in the storm, and soon we were on our way for the next adventure. We moved *Happy Ours* from the marina out to the anchorage for an early morning departure. We had cleared customs and immigration and were bound for Bocus Del Toro, Panama.

Despite the glowing forecast, we made it only as far as the breakwater and seeing the nasty breaking waves, turned around and returned to anchor for another day.

The following day, *Happy Ours* danced confidently over the big wake of one of the ships entering the breakwater, came head to the wind just outside the channel, and rolled out all three sails. The first fifty miles were a sailor's dream—all the perfectly trimmed sails were drawing in the fifteen-knot winds as we glided along with seas on our stern quarter.

At about sunset, rainsqualls appeared with their unpredictable winds and blinding rain showers. It never got better, after many sail adjustments during the night, we finally doused the sails and for the last fifty miles, motored into intermittent rain, heavy seas, twenty-eight knot head winds and a two knot counter current. It took the strong turbocharged engine of our Island packet to make it into port—we made it in thirty hours and used thirty gallons of fuel.

Our contingency plan had been to duck into Bluefield lagoon but it failed because of dangerous reefs and poor visibility. When you can't see clearly, it is best to stay in the open ocean, no matter how much you would like to get in. We had heard stories about sailboats with smaller engines actually turning around and returning to Colon in these conditions and now we understood why.

We made it into Bocus del Toro before dark and safely anchored in a quiet little bay adjacent to Bocus Marina. There are hundreds of quiet little anchorages here to explore; however, our immediate need was rest. Our chart showed an island near where we anchored but we never found it and were a bit concerned that we really weren't anchored in the right spot. Our worries were put to ease when an old friend (Chip on *Felica Lee Felica La*) dinked over to welcome us. He told us the island sank a few years ago and was now a mere shoal spot in the bay.

We also learned that the Port Captain was a bit ill tempered and would fine us for an after hour check in. We decided to take a chance and appear at his office the next morning and claim we had just arrived; however, we left the yellow quarantine flag flying from our starboard spreader just incase we were checked. Luckily, our plan worked and the next day, we checked in with no trouble.

Bocus del Toro is a tiny little resort town full of dive and surf shops, restaurants, bars, and Chinese run grocery stores. Basic supplies were plentiful and only a short mile-long dinks ride away.

We enjoyed being on anchor and sailed in calm waters to neighboring locations where we swam in clear, warm waters and explored the islands. A big problem in this paradise were the little insects called "no seeums" that came out in late afternoon and showed us no mercy as they feasted on our flesh. We found no defense against them other than covering exposed skin.

When it was time to fly home for a visit, we took a slip in Bocus Marina, a very nice facility with concrete floating docks and caring management. They arranged for a water taxi to pick us up and take us to a nearby island with an airport. From there, a short ride in a poorly maintained, overcrowded plane took us back to Panama City where we boarded a large jet for the trip to the U.S.

Some friends in Florida (Phil and Jo Ann Doolady) picked us up at the airport and we caught up on old times until they drove us to Jacksonville where we all attended the Power Squadron annual meeting there.

Norma had been in quite a bit of pain with her arthritic knees for the past year and had received various ineffective treatments from doctors in several different countries. She had gone as far as she could, we needed to help her up from the table after a meeting, and called Colleen (our daughter) to make her an appointment with a specialist in St Louis, which was our next stop.

We took turns riding from Florida to St. Louis with Power Squadron friends Kent and Tracy Simpson and Ed and Rosemary Bialeckie. This gave us a chance to catch up on all the gossip and it was great fun to be with each of them.

Ed dropped us off at our daughter's home in O Fallon, Missouri where we planned to stay for a couple of weeks, then take Amtrak to KC. Rick and Colleen, and the twins (Corey and Courtney) gave us a warm welcome and it was really good to see them.

During Norma's first doctor's appointment, she was treated to painful injections in her knees and when that only offered temporary relief, she was referred to another specialist. She was not yet on Medicare and a large part of our cruising budget had been spent to maintain health insurance. Thank goodness, we maxed out our deductible the first week!

The next specialist re-x-rayed and ran other test only to determine both joints were bone on bone. Norma was given a choice between life with pain and in a wheelchair or having both knee joints replaced.

We returned to our daughters in shock. Rick and Colleen were very supportive and insisted we stay with them while this was taken care of. The following day, we called and reluctantly scheduled the surgery.

We knew friends that had one replacement done and would not go thru having the second one done because of the pain. Another friend was nearly crippled after this procedure and we worried that our sailing lives were over. Norma insisted to having both knees replaced at the same time and the doctor reluctantly agreed that it might be the right thing for her to do.

I looked into renting a car for several months and was astonished at the cost of renting even a sub compact. It seemed a better option to buy a good use car and sell it when it was time to leave.

We had tickets to fly from KC back to Panama on American Airlines and they were very kind in letting us re-schedule without penalty. Next, I called Chuck, the dock master at Bocus Marina. He kindly agreed to extend our use of the dock for as long as needed and promised to keep an eye on *Happy Ours*.

We took our first train ride and went to Lee's Summit where our niece Julie and her daughter Sidney, picked us up at the little station and took us to Mom's in Independence. We used her car to shop for our own and were seeing only high mileage junk in our price range. Finally, Colleen found us a 1991—4 cylinder, 5 speed Pontiac Grand Am with only 49,000 miles on it. The car was immaculate and even had an extended warranty with road service included. We returned to St Louis and purchased that little jewel and used it to visit friends, family and doctors while waiting for the day of the surgery.

The surgery date was stepped up and by early April, Norma had two new knees. Rehab was very painful and began the day after surgery. They had her standing beside the hospital bed— but only for a moment. She progressed nicely and soon returned to Rick and Colleen's where she continued in-house rehab.

Family helped me take very good care of her and it was soon time for more intense therapy at a local athletic enhancement center. She quickly graduated from using a walker to a few days with a cane, then to walking on her own. The grand kids and I saw to it that she walked each day in their neighborhood, enjoying the beautiful spring weather.

The extension on our airline tickets was running out and we needed to return to Bocus del Torro. We had been gone nearly 6 months by then and were anxious to be back onboard *Happy Ours*.

I couldn't stand to sell our little red car and made arrangements to store it in a cave at a cost of only five hundred dollars/year. We purchased a cover to protect the finish and felt confident it would be perfectly safe.

Old friends Gene and Donna Banahan drove us to the airport in K.C. and off we were for more adventure, having promised the doctor to return in one year for a follow up.

When we returned to *Happy Ours*, we found her safe and sound. Unfortunately, un-skilled workers had made a mess of the teak and had spilled varnish everywhere. Apparently they had not used tape and failed to clean up where varnish had run down the hull. I showed Chuck the mess and he sent us a crew to clean varnish off the fiberglass. It took two men three days to clean up the mess. He also refunded our money for the varnish job and apologized. I could have asked for nothing more and really appreciated his concern.

We fixed Norma up a small ladder, suspended by rope to help her swing her tender legs over the lifelines and we walked the island daily. Someone told us about an old, rundown German cemetery that was hidden on the top of the hill behind the marina and went in search of it. Sure enough, it was there and more spooky and run down than we had imagined. Stone vine covered walls had collapsed and were lying in disarray in the weeds. Ornamental black wrought iron gates hung at odd Angels from their rusty hinges and the old tombstones jutted crookedly from the earth as disfigured statues of Angels looked on. Dracula could have wanted for nothing more! All of this was in stark contrast to the beautiful view of the anchorage not a half-mile away.

Bocus was full of yachts we had known in the past and potlucks and Mexican Train Dominos kept us entertained. It was good to be back!

A change in immigration procedures allowed us to stay indefinitely; however, we were told to go Changuinola and obtain a mariner's card and that it would need renewed each month that we were there for a small fee.

Changuinola was a nice little town on the mainland with it's own hospital and shopping and was about an hour's water taxi ride away. A small water taxi would pick us up in Bocus Marina and take us to the main taxi terminal on the island of Bocus Del Toro, where we transferred onto another water taxi to enjoy it's wild excursion across some open water and finally thru the entrance of a small river. We all hung on as it wound its way up the river, thru heavy vegetation with pretty little white flowers, then on to the terminal in Changuinola. A land-based taxi would then pick us up and drive thru the rough roads of a banana plantation, finally dropping us off in town.

One day after taking care of immigration, Norma and I went to the hospital to check on some dizziness problems she started having. The hospital seemed old and was all on one floor. The staff spoke no English and we were lucky to find one doctor with whom we could communicate. We were directed to the waiting room and checked in at the front desk and soon it was our turn to see the Doctor. She charged us nothing for the visit, explaining that Norma was over 65 and that the government would take care of the bill.

Discovering high blood pressure was the problem, she gave Norma a pill and told us we couldn't leave until Norma went to the bathroom, then had her blood pressure re-checked. In the meantime we were to take our prescriptions to the hospital pharmacy, have them filled, then take one of the medicines to the hospital clinic where we were instructed to pay at the casher and wait for Norma to get a shot. This all was really confusing because no one spoke

English and we didn't exactly know where everything was so by the time we arrived for the injection, Norma was mentally drained.

A little fellow in a white coat directed us into a small room and told us to wait while he prepared the injection. When it was ready, he squirted a small amount of the medicine from the needle and spoke a barrage of unintelligible words. Norma blinked and asked, "What did he say?" In jest, I told her to drop her drawers, bend over and grab her ankles and before I could stop her, she did just that!

"No, no Senoria, no nessita!" he exclaimed as he began to laugh. Norma turned red as a beet and scowled at me as she pulled up her britches and tried to re-gain her composure. When he finally stopped laughing, he had her set down on the examining table, rolled up her sleeve, wiped her arm with alcohol, and gave her the shot. I knew I was in trouble and kept my mouth shut as I listened to all the get even things that were going to happen to me.

We sat in the main lobby near the restroom awaiting nature's call and watched as a burley police officer conducted his handcuffed prisoner thru the hallway and seated him beside us. That speeded up the process and Norma soon was ready to get her blood pressure re-checked.

It was now under control and we were allowed to leave. We still had time to catch up with our friends for some shopping, which put Norma in a better mood.

The following week we returned to the hospital for a follow up and for Norma to get a second injection. We heard some hushed giggles starting with the receptionist as we checked in at the clinic and Norma was again mortified. The same little fellow in the white coat greeted us with a big smile and this time things went much smoother; however we were both glad not to have to return.

As usual, our Grunert cold plate refrigeration system failed and we found a technician to repair it once again. Thank goodness we had installed an Adler Barbour air-cooled system in one of the boxes (*Happy Ours* has two) as a refrigerator and small freezer. It kept our box at about forty degrees and the freezer compartment could freeze ice and a small amount of meat—all for only five amps an hour, for about twelve hours a day. Most importantly, I was able to install it myself and it hasn't failed in more than four years.

Our biggest maintenance item was the five kw Northern Lights generator. It had worked flawlessly for years and had become an old faithful friend we always relied on. When we returned to Bocus, the main engine started but the generator motor would not.

Our old friend Jack came up with a maintenance manual for the generator, called his son in law who used to live in David to find out which was the best machine shop. The girls were anxious to go shopping in David while we scrounged around for tools and parts.

The description of the outcome is best described in an article I wrote for a Power Squadron publication:

Why Engine Maintenance?

Norma and I left Happy Ours *in Bocus Del Toro, Panama last Feb to attend the annual meeting in Jacksonville and visit with friends and family for a six week trip to the States. Every thing was working fine on Happy Ours and we were planning on doing just a few cosmetic things before heading North upon our return.*

Six months (not six weeks) later, we returned to Bocus with Norma's two new knees. Happy Ours looked great and we were excited to get back to cruising – only to find the generator wouldn't start. Having exhausted all of my basic knowledge, I looked to our friends for help, all to no avail. We then hired a mechanic on one of the cruising boats who would not get paid unless the generator started – he left a week later with empty pockets just shaking his head.

Our next failure was to hire a local mechanic who had the injector pump and injectors rebuilt to the tune of $650. The generator still wouldn't start so he removed the head, claimed to have rebuilt it but that didn't help. Next he decided the starter wasn't spinning fast enough and had it rebuilt to the tune of $60 – still no joy. After 2 and half months, He gave up and simply quit answering his phone.

We were desperate, the only time I removed a piston from an engine was when it blew out the side of our lawnmower. The only official training I have had was the engine maintenance course with the Power Squadron.

Finally one of the cruisers on a British Yacht (John on SECOND WIND) told me it was time to suck it up and tear the engine apart myself and see what the problem was. He offered to help, so the next day found us in separate compartments tearing the generator into a hundred pieces. It didn't take long to discover that the rings were stuck on two of the three pistons. There was not enough compression to start the 3-cylinder engine.

Jack, on MYSTIC ADVENTURE offered the use of his maintenance and parts manuals and Darold on Moonstruck *offered to get the parts we needed, as he was a Northern Lights distributor in Clear Lake, Texas.*

While waiting for parts, Norma and I took a 1hour water taxi ride, then a 4 hour bus ride to a neighboring city called David where I purchased a torque wrench and some other tools needed to re-assemble the generator. Oh yes, when we pulled the head, we found the valves were in bad shape and needed to be replaced. A very nice lady named Lola took us by van to a large machine shop who, in turn, sent us to an auto parts store to purchase Toyota valves and Nissan seals--they took the head repairs from there.

Getting the parts took about three weeks, and two days of hard work later, Sonny on ANOMONLY came over and adjusted the valves, installed the valve cover and for the first time in almost a year, we once again heard the purr of our little 3 cylinder generator.

Did the Engine Maintenance course help? Didn't hurt!

The maintenance having been taken care of, it was time for Norma to test her new knees on a field trip. We were sick with grief, having just heard that Darin Willoughby, son of our friends Paul and Linda had recently died in an accident back in K.C. He had grown up with our daughter and was very much like a son. There was nothing we could do and we needed to get our minds on something else.

Together with Jack and Jo, our favorite travel companions from days gone by, we went to David, hired a driver and headed for the mountains to the nearby towns of Volcan and Boquete. Each town was home to beautiful flowers, mountain scenery and cool temperatures.

In Boquete, we visited an animal refuge, gardens and an interesting butterfly place, which had been built by a couple of Brits. They built this place from scratch and had imported four little fairy statues from home to decorate the grounds. To their amazement, the Panamanian children visitors were scared to death of the things—similar little creatures were said to hang out in the mountains and jungle, where they devoured little kids. Who would have guessed!

For me, the main attraction was a place called the Barrels. It got its name from some barrel like rocks that were used about eleven thousand years ago as wheels to move heavy stones. Countless artifacts were on display, reflecting both African and Asian cultures. Next to an abandoned, but productive archeological dig was a stream that appeared to flow up-hill towards the mountains and an ancient inactive volcano.

There were fascinating magnetic rocks with smooth flat surfaces inscribed with faces that only appeared when the rocks were wet, picture writings, strange plants, and various implements including a stone device that would grind corn almost by perpetual motion.

All of this was on a private farm and the owner told us many Mystics had visited there to bathe in the uphill stream and gather power from the magnetic rocks.

Norma and Jo liked all of these things but went wild when Lola showed them the wholesale club type store in David. With Lola's membership, they purchased meat and other items, which Lola would freeze and later ship to Bocas for a small fee.

The new knees worked well and we started planning our next trip, which would be to Costa Rica by bus. We started our journey by getting Norma up early (not an easy task) and boarded a water taxi to Bocus town. Together with our friends Jack and Jo, their son

Rob and his wife Wendy, we boarded another water taxi that took us on the wild ride up the jungle river to Changuinola.

Here we found some empanadas for breakfast and took a land taxi to the local bus pickup. The bus took us to a little boarder town where we were unloaded and sent to clear out of Panama. We were then instructed to walk across a rickety old railroad bridge spanning a river that marked the boundary between the two countries.

After filling out some papers and clearing in to Costa Rica, We re-boarded the bus and spent the next 4.5 hours enjoying the beautiful scenery—almost! The bus broke down on a steep mountain road, jumping, leaping, and gasping its final breath; leaving all of us standing with our luggage off on the roadside.

One by one, other buses stopped and picked up a few of us at a time. It was standing room only on the already crowded bus that picked us up but we were glad to be on board. A few gentlemen offered their seats to Norma, Jo, and Windy and joined us men to hang on for dear life as the driver took the mountain curves much too fast, trying to make up time.

Upon our arrival at the San Jose, Costa Rica bus terminal, we found a van to deliver us to our respective destinations. Norma and I stayed at the Posada de Museo Hotel right down town. It is a delightful place, neat and clean, with a great staff. The only drawback is the 6:15 a.m. train that passes near and without shame, blows its horn loudly each morning.

Jack, Jo, Rob, and Wendy stayed long enough to enjoy a good supper with us at the Grand Hotel, then continued on to attend a show at the National Theater. Afterwards, they went to a hotel near the airport where they were to see Rob and Windy off the next morning.

There are many museums in San Jose, Gold, Jade and the National museum as well. Lots of restaurants, the National Park, and the National Theater, are all don't miss things to do and see.

From San Jose, we booked an all day tour that included breakfast at a coffee farm, Poas Volcano and cloud forest, Waterfalls, lunch at the Rain forest lodge, Sarapiqui jungle river boat tour and a drive back thru Braulio Carrillo Park.

What a day! The Volcano is an active water filled crater with steam coming out and beautiful scenery all around. Wildlife on the river was plentiful and included a large fresh water gator that said hello as he lazily ambled along the bank next to us.

After spending a few days in San Jose, we found transportation to Arenal Lodge and couldn't believe how bad the roads were. Jack, Jo, Norma and I were forced to take upgraded rooms at the lodge at no extra cost because ours were not ready. What a shame! We were given mini suites overlooking the beautiful gardens, pool, and the smoking volcano that loomed in the background. Norma woke at 3:45 in the morning to witness a small eruption, complete with a bright red lava flow running down the side of the mountain - all just outside our rear window.

That was to be the end of our watching the volcano as on the following days it disappeared into a dream like cloud, allowing us only brief glimpses of its beauty.

Many tours were offered from the lodge. One of the favorites was the canopy tour where you can ride a basket up the mountain and back, enjoying the panoramic view. The more adventurous (Jack) put on a harness and zipped down the mountain and thru the woods at fifty-five miles per hour on a series of steel cables.

The other favorite was a river adventure. We went down the Rio Frio almost to the boarder. This river trip featured so many caimans, fish, lizards, bats, birds, sloths, monkeys, turtles, Coatimundis, and insects that I ran the battery down on our camera trying to document it all. I got close enough to one of those gator rascals that he splashed mud and water on me when I asked him to smile.

There is a lizard called "The Jesus Christ Lizard" that gets its name from literally running across the top of the water. I'm not that fast but I think I could run him a close second if I ever fell into that infested river!

Leaving the Lodge in Arenal, we took a van to a boat, crossed Arenal Lake, boarded another van, and wound up in Monte Verde. The roads were much worse; otherwise, we still enjoyed spectacular views, cloud forests, and lots of tourist's type stuff.

With the help of our driver, we found a beautiful, secluded place to stay with a view of both the Pacific Ocean and the mountains (Hotel Los Jardines). Weather was cold, rainy, and windy so we went to a frogertarium and looked at frogs. Next, we found the insect place where we looked at a large selection of bugs and spiders. Jack and I talked about seeing the snakes next, which immediately started the " let's go shopping," howl from the ladies.

A couple of days in Monte Verde were enough so we boarded the bus and were back in San Jose for cocktails that evening. We finished off seeing the museums and parks during the next couple of days and then headed back to Bocus Del Toro, Panama.

It was a great trip and we would recommend Costa Rica as an interesting ten-day vacation spot. Norma did well with her new knees and now had confidence to enjoy more fun.

Below is a list of friends that were in Bocus at the same time we were. It is far from complete; however, it was fun looking thru old boat cards and trying to remember names:

Joan and Dan on *Mainly*
Jack and Jo on *Mystic Adventure*
David and Terry on *Sylvester*
Randy and Cheryl on *Caribee*
Geoffrey and Nancy on *Panache*
John and Betty on *Second Wind*
Paul and Malinda on *Daydream*
Patrick and Paula on *Barefoot*
Tom and Susan on *Limerick*
Greg and Judy on *Lone Star Love*
Rankin and Sandy on *Heart of Texas*
Chuck and Pam on *Helen Louise*
Dan and Denise on *Canace*
Bob and Peggy on *Adagio*
Bob and Marilyn on *Zippidee Du*
Paul and Mary on *Angel Heart*
Lynne and Lois on *Spice Island Lady*
Brad and Karen on *Karen's Way*

Steve and Pam on *Viva*
John and Suzanne on *Zeelander*

We celebrated Christmas and New Years in Bocus del Toro. Christmas parades in town were cute, with all the children in the area dancing their way thru the streets.

New Year's Eve was a strange event—we all went to the marina bar, had a few drinks in the presence of scarecrow looking fellow, stuffed with straw. One by one we placed something that represented our troubles from the now ending year in his pockets and at Midnight, he and our troubles were consumed by a blazing fire as we joined hands and danced around the fire in a circle. I had placed a salt encrusted ring from our generator in his shirt pocket, realizing that this was an old ritual of sympathetic magic that had lived on for centuries. I certainly hoped that our generator troubles were over!

Soon it was time to move on. *Mystic Adventure* was ready as well and we left together, the two old boats seemed to enjoy each other's company, traveling along at about the same speed with the knowledge that a friend was close by listening to the VHF.

Chapter 15

The Western Caribbean

Our first destination was San Andres, a beautiful Columbian island an overnight's sail north of Bocus. Being a close reach all the way allowed us to easily motor sail to this isolated wonderland.

On arrival, we checked in and then took an interesting tour to Captain Morgan's cave and other points of interest. In a couple of days, we set sail for another Columbian island, Providencia. We found it to be a more isolated version of the first; offering only limited supplies, beautiful views and a couple of cannon atop a hill.

From here, we enjoyed a lively sail in moderate winds. Our destination was an uninhabited reef called the Vivorillos Cays, where we anchored in the middle of nowhere.

On the way, we caught our first sailfish. The Penn Senator reel started screaming out for help and I dashed over and tightened the drag. All of a sudden, a dark shadow broke the surface behind us, resembling a kite, flying high in the air. It dived back into the ocean and almost caused the stiff rod to bend double, slowing our boat speed a full two knots. Many times, I eased and then tightened the drag on the reel, trying to prevent the 50-pound test line from breaking—all the while, bringing the monster closer to *Happy Ours*.

When he would swim back and fourth, he was sufficiently strong to pull the stern around slightly, causing the autopilot to readjust course and the wheel moved wildly back and forth.

A storm was threatening and we still had all three sails up as we tried desperately to reach the safety of the Vivorillos before nightfall.

Catching a fish was secondary to this goal and I refused to reduce sail. Over two hours passed and we were still trying to land this large fish. Finally, he tired out and I was able to bring him along side.

Norma hooked him in the gill with our gaff but wasn't strong enough to bring him aboard. I put on protective fishing gloves and grabbed him firmly by the snout. It took the combined strength of both of us to finally land this monster. We'll never know how much he weighed but he measured a full six feet long.

Removing the cockpit cushions from the downhill side of the boat, I set about trying to filet this fellow and store the meat in zip lock bags; still sailing along at about 8 ½ knots. I was almost finished when it started to rain and a wave bounced the bloody carcass into my lap. That did it—we tossed the remains overboard and proceeded to hose down both the cockpit and me. When that job was completed, it was time to douse the sails and head in to the anchorage to join *Mystic Adventure* and a couple of other yachts.

We announced our good luck and invited everyone in the anchorage to bring a dish and join us for fresh fish. Norma marinated several bags in teriyaki sauce and then put chunks of this delicious fish on skewers for me to cook on the grill.

Everyone in the anchorage attended and we feasted until after dark. As people left, Norma presented them with a bag of fish. We froze most of what was left, our freezer bulging.

During the previous night's fun, we learned of a reef covered with birds and about sharks being prevalent in the area. We launched the dink the following morning and went in search of birds, which were not too hard to find because there were so many of them that the sky was black over the little island.

The shore was nothing but ragged coral and we chose to set our anchor in a little patch of white sand in only 3 feet of water and carefully wade in. The toothy grinning faces of several sharks that had been cleaned of their meat and then cast aside by fisherman greeted us.

The birds were mostly Boobies and Frigates and nearly all of them ignored us as we walked around taking pictures and enjoying their antics, having gotten past the smell and noise.

Keeping a sharp lookout for sharks, we waded back to the dink and looked for other things to explore. Some remains of an old concrete structure and a bunch of wooden traps being stored there by the fishermen was about the extent of it.

That afternoon we joined Jack and Jo for a game of cards and refreshments. Jo loved to make deserts and always had something special on hand for guests. Tired out from the day's activities, we headed back to *Happy Ours* for a good night's sleep.

There was nothing but thirty-foot Deep Ocean behind us for miles and no boats other than *Mystic Adventure* were left in the anchorage so we slept very sound that night. We were enjoying our coffee the next morning and discovered *Mystic Adventure* had moved during the night and was quite a ways in front of us. I called Jack on the VHF and discovered that we had drug anchor and that Jack was right where he was the previous day.

We started the motor and backed down on the anchor and it wouldn't budge. I tried circling to break it loose but that wouldn't work either. When I went on the bow and took all of the scope up, I noticed a large dark gray shadow moving around just five feet below the surface—a shark. I could see a long black line extending from both sides of our anchor for as far as I could see and realized we were hooked on a piece of old, rusty chain. I let out the scope and decided to enjoy being securely anchored until time to go. I also hoped the shark would leave before I would need to dive down and free ourselves. All day long that dark gray shadow was swimming down there every time I looked.

We needed to get going the next morning and Jack and I devised a plan. He brought his dink over and positioned it by our anchor chain while I suited up with one of the dive tanks that we kept on board for just these occasions. Carefully watching for sharks, I dived off the platform on our stern and swam around to the bow, retrieved an end of a rope from Jack, then slowly dumped the air in my BC and descended in a spiral, keeping an eye out for Mr. Shark.

The plow anchor was hooked on an old ship's chain with square, rusty links and it was too heavy for me to lift to free it. I tied a trip line to a bar on the back of the anchor designed for that purpose. Next, I headed for the dive platform and got out of the water. Jack secured his end of the line to the back of the dink while Norma started our engine.

The little dink motor howled in protest but after a couple of tries it was apparent we were free and being toed slowly by Jack's dink. I don't remember cheering but we all felt like it. I had priced the anchor in an old catalog and discovered it would cost over one thousand dollars to replace—shark be damned!

We immediately set sail for Guanaja, Honduras and enjoyed a quick and easy overnight sail. The recommended anchorage was a long, wet dink ride from town and we decided that taking both dinks would be more comfortable. Guanaja is a fascinating place, built on stilts, with canals running thru it. We found the customs agent and checked into Honduras for the first time. Supplies were limited; however, we purchased enough to get us by and spent the rest of the afternoon enjoying the sites.

Our next stop was at Port Royal, once a pirate stronghold. Being protected by reefs and mountainous terrain, it has only one easily defended entrance. Now, most every thing is private property with mansions surrounding the lagoon. We dinked over to a dock with a for sale sign and were invited by the caretaker to tour the house. It was beautiful and well out of our price range.

One wall was covered with shelves displaying artifacts dug up during the construction of the house. Strangely shaped glass rum bottles and various implements used by the pirate households adorned the shelves. We learned this is where many pirates brought their families to live. There are still stories of buried treasure and I noticed a very expensive metal detector resting in a corner of one of the spacious rooms.

The caretaker was a sailor himself and understood that we could use his Internet access and offered it freely. We enjoyed his company and when we got acquainted, he confessed to turning out with his neighbors to watch the show we had put on trying to drop Jack's headsail so Jo could mend it. After making the repair, a strong wind gust spun us around his anchor before we could roll the big sail back in. We thought no one would notice and hoped they didn't hear the cussing that went with it.

Next, we sailed into French Harbor in Roatan. We loved this beautiful anchorage and made full use of the hospitality offered us by a nearby five star diving resort. Many people from Europe were there to explore the beautiful reefs and enjoy the wonderful weather.

We were more interested in free Internet access, cool drinks and touring this fascinating island. The entire place was up scale and beautiful. Modern grocery stores offered things we had been only dreaming of and the tour we took convinced us this would be a wonderful place to live. We spent as much time here as we dared, then sailed south to La Ceiba on the mainland.

We had only a sketch chart of the entrance and some waypoints from a friend, and were a little uncertain about going in. At about thirty minutes before time to enter, the wind shifted and wave action quickly picked up, causing breaking on shore waves to crash against the breakwater and fly high into the air. As we bounced along, Norma took the helm and I busied myself with the task of rolling in the sails and securing lines.

Norma had no sooner rounded the breakwater than I spotted the jagged remains of a black steel hull protruding from the water directly in our path. She hadn't spotted it yet and when I told her to turn to port, she stated we were right on course. Disaster was way to close to argue and I screamed " Damn it, turn NOW". She then did as I directed and we both shivered as *Happy Ours* scooted past the ugly black hull with only feet to spare.

It wasn't over; however, and our new course led us thru water so shallow that the waves began bouncing *Happy Ours* mercilessly off the bottom, then rolled her precariously on her side.

Fearing that we might suffer the same fate as the poor obstruction, I yelled at Norma to put on full power. This time there was no argument and black smoke poured from our diesel exhaust as our startled engine came to full rpm as Norma gained control and steered back into the deeper part of the entrance. She had saved our boat that day—there was nothing I could have done to get back to the helm and help her in time. I smiled at our Hero and noticed she was shaking so badly that she could hardly stand and had not thought to cut back on the throttle. When I asked her to throttle back, she did and then told me I needed to take the wheel for a while.

I don't remember if our friends on *Mystic Adventure* ever saw the underwater obstruction, but they missed it entirely and even though we saw their keel nearly out of the water a time or two, their larger 49' boat went in with out a hitch.

Happy Ours headed up a little jungle river off the bay to stay in Lagoon Marina, while *Mystic Adventure* stopped at the haul out yard to get a new bottom paint.

We were fascinated with our new surroundings; exotic trees and sounds hypnotized us as I steered *Happy Ours* around a bend of the river, discovering a little marina along the bank. It looked out of place in the jungle atmosphere; we half expected to see Humphrey Bogart in the *African Queen* coming from the other direction instead of the tall mast of modern day yachts and couldn't wait to explore this wonderful place.

Our old friend Mitch from *Lone Star Love* was there helping Rita, the owner, with the marina because her husband had been shot to death earlier that year. Beautiful jungle variety plants and flowers surrounded the grounds and there was a clean swimming pool for us to enjoy.

The work being done, Jack and Jo joined us at the marina and we made plans for a five-hour bus trip to visit the Copan Mayan ruins.

Copan is an old town in a rural community of Honduras. Most of the men wear western boots and white straw cowboy hats and it feels like being in a small town in Missouri. The streets; however, were stone and the grades were steep. Very little English was spoken here and we relied on our Spangelish to get us buy.

The major attractions were Tucan Mountain and the Copan ruins. The Mayans covered up their old temples about every 52 years and built new, in honor of the new kings. Tunnels have been dug to access the prior temples, which seem mostly intact, protected by being underground. Only two levels have been excavated and there is much work for archeologists to do here. Pyramids were well preserved and we certainly had not wasted our money on this trip. Huge deep-rooted trees known as La Ceibas had been considered sacred by the Mayans and stood as monuments among the ruins to this lost civilization.

Tucan Mountain offered a walking trail, which was surrounded by cages that were home to exotic birds. At the end of the trail, we were surprised to find the birds no longer in cages and the guides would one at a time set these beautiful creatures on our arms and shoulders for pictures.

Jack and I learned of some isolated ruins located on a farm not far from where we stayed and talked the girls into joining us on this final outing. We were told that there was a trail leading to what remained of the home of a well to do Mayan family and declining paying for the services of a guide, struck out on our own in search of the ruins. The trail was easy to follow as we walked on past the little stone ruin and proceeded to get lost in the steamy jungle. At the end of the trail, we climbed a steep hill, clinging on to tree roots and rocks as we progressed to the top where we found a lonesome road.

Red-faced with heat and exhaustion, we found some children along the road and after buying some of their handcrafts; we were directed back the way we had come. On the way back down, we finally spotted the elusive ruins, hardly more than a pile of rocks. A couple of stones had what resembled frogs carved on them and that was about the extent of it. Needles to say the girls weren't happy with us and the trip back wasn't all that pleasant, but we had another story to tell.

The ride back to the boat was in a first class air-conditioned coach and we enjoyed the scenery as it rolled past our windows. The cameras were full of pictures and we had now seen our first Mayan pyramid.

Our plan was to spend the upcoming hurricane season tucked safely in Guatemala, several miles up the Rio Dulce. The only problem was that with our near 6ft drafts, we could only cross the sand bar across the river entrance at high tide that only occurred a few days a month.

Jack and I carefully studied the tide tables of the Rio Dulce we had previously downloaded from the internet and determined we might still have time to visit the third out island—Utila, just a short sail away.

Utila had its own character, nowhere near as attractive as Roitan had been, yet still full of restaurants, bars, boaters and tourists. We walked the main street, taking in the sights along the way, then found the office where we could clear out of Honduras. This done, we returned to our boats and prepared for our next day's trip.

We spent the next night tucked in to Puerto Escondito, then on around to Cabo Tres Puntas the following day where we staged our entrance to the Rio Dulce—only an hour's sail away. We were a little concerned about going in there as we had heard the drug lords had taken over the town where we needed to check in and took all of the police and officials hostage just a couple of weeks earlier. Things were supposed to be back to normal but nothing is ever for sure.

Chapter 16

Guatemala

Crossing the bar in the mouth of the Rio Dulce with our six-foot drafts required that we arrive at the entrance with the tide up and preferably still rising. Each of us had several sets of way points given to us by friends and some directions for lining up on a point of land. Jack and I had selected the points that they all seemed to agree on and that worked for us. Our depth meter read six feet a time or two; however I don't believe we ever touched bottom.

Having passed the bar exam, we carefully motored in shallow water and anchored at Livingston, where we checked in and explored the town. We were directed to an ATM to obtain local currency and as we walked the streets, there was no sign that there had ever been any trouble.

We had been cautioned not to anchor in the river at night—boarding and robberies were common, so we headed up the Rio to a little safe haven called Texan Bay.

The river was a beautiful, providing a new panorama as we rounded each bend. Very steep and tall walls of jungle gave way to flat land as we preceded further inland and it didn't take long before we had reached the place to turn into and stay the night.

A Texan named Mike had some how managed to build a marina and restaurant here and hired some locals to keep it safe. He and his wife were fun to be with and we enjoyed Tex-Mex food and some almost cold beer. A new, larger transformer was to be installed soon, until then; they had to limit electricity usage.

Just to be on the safe side, I set up our little motion detector and securely locked the dink and outboard before retiring for the night.

We always had his and her flair pistols near by as well as an assortment of pepper spray, spear guns, a machete, and a mean tempered wife.

Happy Ours had lockable doors instead of hatch boards, which we locked at night. There were plenty of small ports and hatches for ventilation. Some cruisers installed stainless steel bars on the larger hatches; however, we never really liked the idea of delaying our escape in case of an emergency. We even heard of one yacht with bars was threatened with being burned alive if they didn't open up and that the intruders had sprinkled gasoline on the deck.

A good night's sleep behind us, we enjoyed coffee and a breakfast bar and once again, motored *Happy Ours* out into the river channel. Jungle gave way to clearings with a variety of private homes, shacks, and even a restaurant or two along the way.

Children wearing backpacks were paddling their dugout canoes in route to school and not one of them was wearing a life jacket. Some had wooden boats with small outboard motors and I noticed they kept off to the sides of the river channel for safety.

When we were in Roatan, Mike and Cindy on *Dragon Heart* had advised us that Mario's Marina was as safe as any and had been the hub of social activities for years. Luckily, both Jack and I had made reservations because the place was full when we arrived. We called on the VHF and were given docking instructions and were soon eating lunch and enjoying cold drinks in their nifty out door restaurant and bar.

There was a small grocery store, book and movie swap/rental as well as a swimming pool and TV hut on the premises. Internet was available and Jim, the manager ran a water taxi to town and back for our convenience.

The nearest town was Fronteris, about a two-mile ride by water from our marina. It resembled the old west, with outdoor markets; a main street lined with many little shops and a grocery or two. Hard looking men walked about wearing white straw cowboy hats, jeans and work boots and some of them carried holstered guns on their belts.

Most the women were sun baked and wrinkled from hard farm work but could manage a smile when they greeted us. English was at a premium, and negotiations for fruits and vegetables went a lot better if we spoke Spanish.

Many other marinas lined both banks of the river and hundreds of sailboat masts decorated the skyline. It became a game for Norma and I to count how many boats we recognized as we dinked along to and from town. This was truly the place to be for hurricane season.

We played Mexican Train dominos every Sunday and danced and partied at least once a week. People would come by dink from other marinas to enjoy the restaurant specials, the Saturday swap meets, dominos, dancing, karaoke and special holiday events.

Guatemala city was a scenic five-hour bus ride away and a pleasant change of atmosphere; offering museums, restaurants, and a large Sunday market as well as air-conditioned hotels and an airport. From there we could arrange tours to Flores, Tikal, Pacaya volcano, Antigua, Lake Atitlan, and Panachel.

We tried something different and went with a group of cruisers by bus to the beautiful little town of Flores and then on to Tikal, the most famous Mayan ruins in Guatemala.

The crew of *Second Wind* arranged the trip: David, Claire, and their teen-age daughter Kati. Steve, Gayle, Matthew and David from *La Rina Gayle*, Jack and Jo from *Mystic Adventure*, Bryce and Cindy from *Andante* and Norma and myself all took the water taxi from Marios marina to Fronteris, boarded a public bus and headed for Flores, where we each had reservations at various hotels. We found a centrally located restaurant overlooking the beautiful clear blue waters of a lake and made this our meeting place.

After exploring the shops in this little tourist town, we arranged for a tour of the Tical ruins. The following morning, we boarded a van furnished by a local travel agency and off we went for another adventure. As we walked along the jungle trails that connected various pyramids and temple ruins, we enjoyed the colorful birds and curious monkeys that filled the trees along the way.

We were allowed to climb the towering pyramids and enjoyed breath-taking views from the tops of each, as they peeped out above the trees of the lush green jungle.

Our guide was extremely informative and freely imparted to us his knowledge as we viewed each attraction. By 4 p.m., we were exhausted, hot, and didn't complain when the van pulled up to collect our remains.

We enjoyed another gorgeous sun set dinner and drinks while overlooking the lake, and were soon off to our rooms for a good night's sleep.

We were back on our boats before dark, sorting our pictures and laughing about how it took us twice as long to climb the pyramids as it did the teenagers. Their enthusiasm and excitement certainly added to the enjoyment of our trip and we wished our grandchildren were there to share the experience.

We traveled several times back to Guatemala City; both just the two of us and also with our dear friends Jack and Jo. Jack and I are very much attracted to museums and historical things while our women seem to enjoy shopping, so there was never a time to get bored. We often stayed in a hotel named Los Tores that was cruiser friendly and easy on our pocketbooks as well as being right down town.

We left our boat and flew home for a visit, spending a night in a really scary neighborhood near the airport and vowed to stay at the Los Tores on our return trip. The hotel near the airport literally locked us in behind iron gates and recommended we have fast food delivered in for supper rather than going off premises. The room was dirty and sported what looked like unclean beading – all for a price that was more than Los Tores had been. Management was friendly and accommodating—they even took fresh sheets off a bed in another room and installed them on our own when we complained.

When we returned to *Happy Ours*, we discovered the Rio Dulce was flooded from heavy rains and no power was available in the marina. This meant no air-conditioning and we spent the steamy afternoons in the swimming pool with other cruisers trying to cool off. It took more than two weeks before power could be restored and by then, I was covered with insect bites. They each would produce a small blister and itched like crazy. Scratching was a favorite pastime of several of us cruisers and of course we managed to get an infection so severe that it took a specialist in Guatemala City to figure out a treatment.

He tried several different medicines before finding the right one and had us call him every two weeks for new instructions. Although most of the medicine didn't require a prescription, we found that it was necessary to visit several pharmacies just to obtain enough for a week's treatment. It took six weeks to get rid of the infection and I still have scars on my arms and legs.

Jo on *Mystic Adventure* fell in to the dirty river while cleaning her boat, wounding her ankle on the way down. The marina staff and fellow cruisers saw to it she got to a hospital in a neighboring town where she was told it was only a sprain and nothing was broken.

Her ankle turned black and became very swollen and she finally went to a doctor in Guatemala City where she was given antibiotics; they scraped the dead tissue to the bone and suggested she might need a skin graft.

Her ankle continued to get worse and to save her foot, several of the nurses in the marina insisted she go to the U.S. immediately, where they again removed the dead tissue and performed a skin graft. It all turned out ok but she has a nasty scar of her own.

While we were waiting for hurricanes to pass, we amused our selves by taking a Spanish class at the marina, which was missing two students by the end of the season. They had purchased a sailboat and had spent some time fixing it up. Anxious to see how it would be to live aboard, they motored out of their marina and anchored across the river from us for the night.

They were boarded and he was stabbed to death. She had been stabbed in the chest with a machete and her call for help rang out on VHF radios up and down the river. She was weak and could hardly talk but help was soon on the way. A fellow that called himself the jungle medic as well as several nearby cruisers responded and was able to save her.

This, coupled with a boarding and robbery we heard about up river, triggered a chain of events that went on for several weeks. The military came and surrounded the village behind our marina, arresting some people thought to be involved.

For the next few nights, gunfire echoed up and down the river as a vigilante type justice system took over. No one wanted a military presence in this opportunistic community. We learned that a woman and her eighteen-year-old son, who were thought to be fencing the things stolen in the robberies, had been shot to death in a neighboring marina in a brutal execution style shooting.

Patrol boats, once non-existent, ran up and down the river and the healing process began—too late to help our friend and his wife, but maybe not too late to help the rest of us.

Violence didn't end however; the nice little guard in our marina was murdered just outside the gate coming from the village behind us and we were told it had been and un-related incident. His coffin sat on the dock in front of *Happy Ours* in the very same place he used to stand as he tried to understand my Spanglish. His family and friends assembled at the marina and waited for the pontoon boat to carry him to his final resting place in town.

Shortly afterwards, Norma and I were preparing for bed when we heard the unmistakable blast from a shotgun just next to our boat. We doused the lights and hit the floor, cowering as far below the waterline as possible. When all was quiet, we checked the locks on our doors and went to bed, weapons in hand. We learned the next day that marina security spotted someone trying to board a boat that was anchored behind *Happy Ours* and fired a warning shot to scare them off. I was glad to hear they were on the job.

Anxious to escape this environment, Jack, Jo, Norma and I made a final trip to Guatemala City and finished up sight seeing by touring Panachel and lake Atitlan—a beautiful blue water lake surrounded by mountains. This was definitely a tourist area; however, not too many Americans seemed to venture that far.

While there, we scheduled a trip to an active volcano, which overlooks Guatemala City and the surrounding towns. We had heard it was a difficult climb and decided to take horses up the mountain. Norma opted out (thank God) for fear of injuring her knees, leaving Jack, Jo and myself to go it alone.

The first part of our journey was easy and fun—the horses did all of the climbing. The trail became so steep that we literally lay against the horses' necks and held on for dear life. Finally, we reached a little flat place where we were instructed to dismount.

We noticed a black mountain top looming against the evening sky ahead of us and saw a small trail leading to the top with people appearing to be the size of ants climbing upward. We didn't know that the last hour and a half of the climb was considered too dangerous for the horses and we needed to proceed on foot. It had become pitch black before we reached the top, with only the city lights illuminating the horizon and the red glow of molten lava ahead. The black lava rock was sharp and crumbly and it took its toll on our bare skin as we clawed our way upward.

Arriving at the top, we could see the red glow of lava thru cracks and the rocks we walked on were hot enough to melt the rubber soles of my deck shoes. Our guide took his walking stick and stirred it around in the molten lava. It quickly burst into flames and he used it to light a cigarette. I was impressed!

The wind was gusting at about twenty-five bone-chilling knots and the footing was unsteady, especially on the way down in the dark. The guide caught Jo and carried her down the trail almost under his arm, leaving Jack and me alone. We finally reached the horses and I really felt sorry for those that chose to do the whole trip on foot. The ride down was beautiful, my horse carefully chose a safe path as I relaxed my tired muscles and just enjoyed the breath taking view.

It was nearly ten p.m. before we were returned to our hotel and we still needed to eat. Norma was both worried and hungry when we arrived at the hotel so we wasted no time in finding a restaurant that was still open. Satisfied with delicious meals under our belts, which had been supplemented by plenty of wine, we literally slept like the dead that night.

The next morning, we ate a hurried breakfast and took a van back to the Rio; excitedly telling our friends of the beautiful, fascinating places we had visited. The next group of cruisers was already making plans to see these places and asked about hotels and tour prices.

All was not well; however, I walked up the little trail to the marina office and noticed small groups of cruisers huddled together talking privately and wondered what was going on.

Finishing my business at the marina, I spotted three women having an animated conversation at the TV room—a cute little thatch covered building used for social occasions at the pool.

Knowing all three pretty well, I strolled over and ask, "Ok, what's been going on around here. Too many people are whispering about something and Norma and I don't want to be left out of anything juicy."

The words had hardly left my big mouth when one of the ladies screamed, "I'll tell you what the blank is going on! That no good blankety blank husband of mine has been blanking around with that fat-assed blankity blank woman from town." All I could do was blink as she continued "I caught them right over there in one of the rental units going at it and the SOB was getting her from behind."

Trying to defuse the conversation, I ask if she was sure it had been him in there. She immediately took out some pictures from her purse, threw them in front of me on the counter, screaming she had caught the SOB red handed and even had the pictures to prove it.

Reluctantly I gathered up the photographs and as she screamed more profanities, I examined the so-called evidence. Sure enough, all three pictures were just as she promised, with my friend—her husband clearly enjoying himself in the unmistakable throes of passion with a very obese female. I could have sworn he was even smiling and posing for the camera!

There being nothing left to say, I just shook my head and walked away vowing never to ask anyone anything like that again. It eventually worked out ok—the intruder was banned from the marina and our friends managed to save their marriage after weeks of negotiations. Too much togetherness in the confines of a marina over a period of time may not be a good thing and if it is possible, leaving the boat and doing inland travel occasionally is advised.

There was a super friendly couple named Bob and Trish on *Barnacle* who had been in the Rio for several years and really knew their way around Guatemala. Bob was a photojournalist and Trish had extensive layman knowledge of the Mayans. With the two of them as our guides, we were given opportunities to see things we had not even heard about and we really enjoyed their company.

They owned a small runabout with a 65hp outboard motor and several times Bob would invite me to explore some of the small rivers that emptied into the Rio Dulce. Knowing my passion for photography, Bob seemed to delight in stopping *Barney* and drift along in the current, not saying a word, until I spotted what he had already recognized as a photographic opportunity. One such shot was a snow-white egret swinging on a vine that was looped down from a tall cliff on the river's edge. With so much to see, some times it took me a minute to spot these things and Bob waited patiently until my picture taking was complete, then smile with satisfaction and throttle up *Barney*.

Trish knew of a little known Mayan ruin not far from the marina called Quirigua and helped a group of us set up a mini tour with her and Bob acting as our guides. That day we saw some of the most beautifully carved jade mask and extremely well preserved examples of stone writings that are available anywhere.

On another trip, they took just the two of us by car to a local beach on the ocean. We were literally the only non-local people there and encountered some curious smiles and greetings. Along the way, they stopped for us to explore a cave, some hot, steaming springs and other points of interest as we drove thru the beautiful countryside.

Perhaps the longest, most unusual river trip was with our friend Mike from Texas Bay Marina. He and Bob were great friends and when Bob found out about a trip Mike was going to take up the Polocheck River, Jack and I were invited to join the small group of explorers. Armed with cameras, drinks and lunch, we climbed into

Mike's boat and headed down river with his friend and bodyguard setting watchfully in the bow, a shotgun on hand in case of trouble. After fueling up, we motored past an old stone fort and then continued on for what turned out to be a fascinating eleven-hour journey in the open boat. It had a very large motor and Mike skillfully moved us along at a good clip so we could finish up in just one day. Carefully searching for the mouth of the river, we eased our way over a bar, then on into the beginning of a narrow, winding channel.

Unspoiled, primitive, and scary beautiful, the river was out of her banks and some levees had given away. Our arrival disturbed the waterfowl guarding the entrance and the sky darkened as we were surrounded by the sounds of a hundred birds taking flight. Our cameras could not capture what our eyes beheld and only provided a pitiful documentation of such an event.

Winding our way up river, we slowed to listen to the angry sound of howler monkeys that seemed to protest our intrusion. Beautiful birds and scenery passed by as Mike continued to pick out the deepest part of the river channel and we continued onward.

Coming around a bin, we spotted a formable looking water buffalo that also didn't seem to enjoy our intrusion into his territory. Lowering his head, his large gleaming horns aimed in our direction, he followed along the riverbank, silently awaiting his chance to challenge our right to be there.

Mike, being from Texas, let out his best imitation of a bull bellowing. Me, being from Kansas City couldn't resist the challenge and followed suit with my best bellow. The incensed buffalo climbed into the water, letting out a real challenge, causing our blood to run cold and Mike to open the throttle to get away from the irritated beast, all the while Bob was taking pictures with his professional style camera.

Proceeding up river, we passed by a lot of flooded farmland, waving at the locals standing on the bank watching the crazy gringos. Next, we encountered a Mayan village, seemingly isolated from the world but still functioning with their own culture.

Every bend offered new scenery but the mountains still loomed in the background, awaiting our arrival. We passed a community of women and children washing clothes in the river and another colorfully clothed group of people attending a sort of wedding ceremony.

When we finally reached the place where the river flowed out between two mountains, the remains of an old concrete bridge that had collapsed into the river stopped us. Jagged concrete protruded from the water, creating little whirlpools and eddies from the swift current. It simply was too dangerous to continue, so we turned around and started retracing our route back down stream. We waved and bellowed at the passing water buffalo and enjoyed our ride along in the swift current, arriving back at the Marina late in the afternoon.

I had hidden a GPS in my backpack and was able to print out our route with the help of Google maps, which I copied and shared with the others—the least I could do in appreciation of such an adventure.

The Rio Dulce could be a dangerous place, but to us it seemed ok as long as we followed the advice of fellow cruisers and some of the locals. We were told never to anchor out in the river at night except for at a few protected locations. We learned it was better to spend our nights having fun in one of the marinas and to avoid going into town. We did not wear expensive jewelry and carried a credit card only when necessary. I used a belt with a hidden zipper to carry extra money and never had any trouble. Blue jeans seemed the manly clothing in town and I often would put my credit card, a copy of my passport, and some money tucked in my socks. I carried only small bills in my pockets and no wallet.

Most of the people were friendly, the ones that weren't, we just left alone but put on the appearance of being prepared to handle trouble if necessary. We found if you walked stooped over, just shuffling along looking at the ground you could appear as an easy target for robbers. Good humor and a smile was a big help—these things worked no matter what the language.

Drugs were popular in Guatemala and our approach to this was just to live and let live. We minded our own business and that worked for us.

Hurricane seasoned had finally ended in November; however, we were having so much fun at Marios that we opted to enjoy the Holidays there with our friends. Boats were brightly decorated and Bob and Trish had installed a six-foot tall inflatable Santa Clause on the bow of their boat, which was parked just in front of the restaurant. This mighty Santa seemed to set the mood thru Christmas, and then deflated into a pitiful red and white plastic ball for the New Years party. The gunfire disappeared, being replaced by music and laughter on the Rio.

Mark and Amie, young kids from *Mema* were on hand to remind us what Christmas was all about and their excitement was contagious. We all shared gifts with some of the children in town and staying a few more weeks certainly had its rewards.

Soon, it was time to leave the Rio and we carefully watched the tide tables to plan crossing the bar. Bob took me to the mouth of the river in *Barney* and I sounded out the entrance with a portable depth sounder, zigzagging back and fourth using the GPS to mark the deepest parts.

Provisioned up, we planned to spend the following day in Texan Bay, ride up to town with them and check out, then leave on the rising tide the next evening, which was just before dark. We made no plans except to travel alone and we cast off our lines early.

We were very surprised when Bob and Trish came alongside in Barney and wished us well as we wound around the bins in the river. We said our goodbyes once again, and then they headed back to Mario's and we proceeded on to see Mike.

We had no sooner arrived at Texan Bay than we heard a call for *Happy Ours* on the VHF. It was Michel and Roy on *Dream Odyssey* and they had resolved the problems with their boat and wanted to travel with us. We agreed to rendezvous, cross the bar together and anchor the following night at Tres Puntas. They were also heading north but didn't seem to want to discuss their plans in detail on the radio. We understood, the Rio was not a good place to advertise your location.

We learned that *Andante* would also be crossing the same night but would need to wait longer for higher tide because of their seven-foot draft. All three of us were going to spend the night at Tres Puntas, but *Andante* would not be going to Belize.

All went well, we touched bottom only slightly, then crossed the bar and headed out, anchoring just at dark with Roy and Michel close by. *Andante* came in later, using our anchor lights as a beacon. They had to have the locals drag them across the bar with a powerboat that was standing by for just such an occasion.

There was no celebration, we didn't even launch the dinks—just ate a light supper, checked our anchors and headed for our bunks. We left the VHF radios set on a pre-determined channel for safety and kept our flair guns handy just in case of trouble but there was none. Another chapter of our lives closed as quietly as it had opened and we were grateful.

Chapter 17

You'd Better Belize It!

Dream Odyssey was a pleasure to sail with. We hoisted our anchors at about the same time, said goodbye to our friends on *Andante*, and then set sail for Punta Gorda in Belize. By the time we arrived, the weather turned nasty and each of us quickly doused our sails and motored in to the harbor.

Soon, the rain ended, winds calmed down, and we dinked to shore in search of customs and immigration. Friendly folks on the dock directed us to the proper buildings where we found the officials waiting (we were the only boats in the harbor).

It was wonderful to clear into a country whose people spoke English. Norma and I had just completed our paperwork, when we heard Roy tell that they had two cats on board. Ignoring the health records presented to them, they assessed a one hundred dollar fine for Roy not having the correct paperwork for bringing the cats into their country. No amount of reasoning with them could cause them to change their minds and Roy finally begrudgingly agreed to pay the money.

We were told where to find an ATM—they could not accept foreign currency so we headed up the street in search of the money machine only to be distracted by the wonderful smell of food coming from a little restaurant along the way.

We quickly obtained some of their currency, returned to pay our fees, then headed out in search of food. Before long, we were wolfing down some real American style cuisine that didn't come with black beans and rice. Roy and Michel were still smarting from the cat paperwork fine but their mood improved quickly as we ate and discussed exploring a new country.

We purchased chips for our telephones, exchanged the new information with each other, and then wandered the town finding some limited supplies.

Even though we had been advised not to stay the night in this open anchorage, the weather was beautiful and we stayed in town almost until dark, leaving no time to travel. Sure enough, during the night, a storm developed and caused a very uncomfortable situation for sleeping. The boats rocked violently as the waves came rolling in from the ocean and I spent most of the night doing anchor watch. The next morning, weather had cleared somewhat and we anxiously headed out in search of a better place to stay with another approaching front forecasted.

Rounding Wilson's Cay, we tucked into a beautiful, isolated bay behind Icacos Point. It took about four hours to travel the twenty miles and when we dropped the anchors, all of us were ready for a nap.

The weather forecast proved accurate and the wind howled, bringing torrential rain off and on for the next five days. We discovered the passion Roy and Michel had for playing cards as well as Mexican Train Dominos and spent many hours laughing as we enjoyed each other's company.

It had been *Dream Odyssey* that was boarded and robbed in the Rio Dulce about the time the cruisers had been attacked across from our marina and I carefully asked if they would share with us the story of when this happened. At first both of them hesitated, just looking at each other until finally Michel started speaking. I could tell how difficult it was for them to talk about it and really appreciated their sharing the horrible experience.

They were new to the Rio Dulce and had just checked in that morning. They were traveling with two other boats and had asked the customs agent if it was ok to anchor in the river for the night before proceeding to their marinas. He didn't think there was any problem with it and didn't discourage them from doing so.

Anchored in a beautiful place along the river with their friends not far away, Roy and Michel went below to enjoy dinner and a movie.

Their large old Morgan 51 was very comfortable and so stable that they never felt the intruder's presence until one of them put a machete to Michel's throat, tapped her on the shoulder and said "Hola". There were five robbers in all, one armed with a gun.

Roy and Michel were bound hands and feet behind them and watched helplessly as their beautiful boat was torn apart and robbed. Not knowing their fates, Michel worked her bindings loose in an attempt to escape only to be discovered by one of the bandits. She was re-tied, this time more carefully and the robbers continued their evil work.

The dingy was securely locked on the back of the boat and one robber demanded that Roy give him the keys. Too upset to remember where the keys were, Roy and Michel were unable to tell them. Making angry, threatening jesters the robbers finally gave up and moved on.

Michel flushed with anger as she told us one of the robbers came to her when they were ready to leave and told her she was a good woman. It was best her hands were still tied, as I believe she would have attacked him.

After the robbers left, it took some time for Roy and Michel to get free and then alert the others who had neither heard nor seen anything.

Even though they filed a report and suspects were apprehended, they only got back three or four of the sixty some odd items that were stolen.

They had given a fellow cruiser permission to write an article about the corruption in the local government regarding this incident. Unfortunately, the article came out about the time we left. They were very much concerned about their safety and did not want to travel alone; neither did they want to spend much time on the VHF radio.

If we needed to use the radio, we used "Dreamy" instead of *Dream Odyssey*, and "Happy" for *Happy Ours*. This was kind of fun and our pseudo names stayed with us all the while we traveled together.

When the weather cleared, our next destination was Placentia; one of those places with white sand beaches, bars, tourist, and expensive restaurants.

Several of our cruising friends were here and it was a pleasure to spend time with them in this safe, pleasant place. One evening, we dinked to shore to find all of the bars packed with locals as well as tourists. Every TV set was turned on and tuned to the same channel and a festive, joyful atmosphere prevailed throughout the town.

We picked a place with an empty table, ordered some drinks and inquired as to why the celebration. The waiter looked at us in disbelief and told us that it was Obama's inauguration and it seemed as if the whole world was rejoicing. We knew an important new chapter of history was unfolding as we sipped our drinks and joined the party.

From Placentia, we sailed to Garbutt Cay, anchored and spent the night. The following day found us sailing in shallow water down to Tobacco Cay, where we again anchored for another night in these colorful surroundings. The next morning found us picking our way thru the reef and finally into open ocean. We sailed on to Long Cay and tucked in behind its reef and prepared for some unsettled weather. Lighthouse reef and the Blue Hole are accessible from here and we dinked ashore to find a dive shop.

Learning that Belize charges about $80 US in park fees to visit the Blue Hole, we decided to just spend $ 20 and enjoy the day exploring Light House Reef. The dive boat dropped us off at Lighthouse while some others continued on to the hole.

We visited a rookery loaded with Frigates and Boobies, swam in the crystal clear water, shelled, explored the old lighthouse ruins, and took pictures of it all as we wandered the beach. The dive boat picked us up and we enjoyed hearing the diver's stories as we bounced along on the way back to Long Cay. They told us that we had been wise not to spend an additional $ 80 for a fairly lackluster dive experience. "It would have been great if you had never dived anyplace else," was the comment that all seemed to agree upon.

On the way back to our boats, we spotted a bright reflection in the water, which, on closer examination turned out to be a dive mask in its case. We decided that it must belong to the people from a large motor yacht named *Bright Star*, which was anchored behind us and took it over to them. As it turned out, the mask had an expensive prescription lens that could not be easily replaced.

The grateful skipper and his wife invited us to enjoy the Super Bowl with them via their satellite TV and new friendships were cemented. We all brought snacks to share as well as something to drink and enjoyed a very nice evening.

When the weather settled down again, we headed to the Drowned Cays to tuck in for yet another front. *Bright Star* and their friends joined us for some more camaraderie, as there seemed plenty of room in this protected anchorage.

The place was not as isolated as it looked—our peace was soon disturbed when a tug boat towing a line of barges came motoring in and proceeded to tie the barges to the mangroves in anticipation of the coming foul weather. The tug continued this process for the next couple of days, providing us with fascinating entertainment like no other.

We soon moved on north, using the shallow inner passage. *Dreamy's* depth finder wouldn't read below ten feet and they opted to let *Happy* lead the way. They later described seeing us leaving a sandy vortex behind as we motored thru the shallow water, with our nearly six-foot draft disturbing the sleeping powdery white bottom.

For miles we nervously watched the depth finder reading six foot as we eased along. At one point, we slid up and over a sandy shoal that literally laid *Happy Ours* on her side but she used her momentum to keep on going. This no doubt disappointed some local boaters that stood by this area, making extra money towing unfortunate yachties off the improperly marked bar.

It was with a sigh of relief that we pulled into Corker Cay and dropped the hook. We were ready for the niceties of civilization and promptly set our dinks in the water, installed the outboard motors, and headed for shore. The trip had been exhausting—fraught with fear of running aground but now that was all behind us. We did it!

We found ourselves in another tourist town with all the trappings; Beaches and bars were everywhere. Surrounded by fun things to see and do nearly put us in overload—quite a contrast from the Drowned Cays.

Together with Roy and Michel, we headed straight for a local restaurant and gorged ourselves with plenty of good things to eat, washed it down with sufficient amounts of wine and cold brewskies and just sat and grinned at each other. It had been a long day.

We met some other cruisers and learned that it was not necessary to take our boats thru the shallow inner passage north to check out. They told us when we were ready; just simply take a water taxi to San Pedro and walk to the customs and immigration office from the terminal. The other option was to cross the reef, sail on the outside and negotiate a confusing, shallow passage through a reef into the harbor. Hearing this, we were delighted and enjoyed a couple of weeks in this paradise without concern.

When our allotted time was up, we simply got our paperwork together and headed for the water taxi office. The ride was enjoyable and in no time we arrived at the pier in San Pedro on Ambergris Cay. Checking out was a breeze in Belize and we spent most of the day enjoying the town. It was really laid back with mostly sand streets and really casual dress. Golf carts were an important transportation medium and the drivers were almost as crazy as the cabbies in New York. We simply weren't use to all this traffic!

We once again provisioned our boats and carefully planned the next leg of our trip. All we needed to do was go back south about eight miles, pick our way thru the reef at Long Cay, find deep water and head north.

It had been nearly five days since checking out and technically, we were in Belize illegally so we all were anxious to get going. The weather simply wouldn't cooperate. On the fifth morning, we left the harbor and headed south, literally bounced across the reef in the nasty eight-foot seas and found deep water. Both boats hoisted sail and began the 250nm trip to Isla Mujeres, Mexico. Seas were running about eight to ten feet and we started out on an easy reach in about twenty knots of wind. We made good about eight knots until the wind died down at dark, then as the wind slowed, so did we. It was a pleasant, uneventful trip until we arrived at Cozumel the following evening, where a really strange thing happened.

Chapter 18

A Strange Welcome to Mexico

We made a wide swing to avoid the naval base at the southern tip of Cozumel, taking advantage of the two knot current prevalent in the area. It had just gotten dark and the wind died so we rolled in our sails, fired up the motor and turned on the running lights.

Dreamy opted to take a short cut, putting them much closer to the southern tip of the island. It was a really dark night and we had lost track of each other. Suddenly, we heard *Dreamy* frantically calling us on the VHF. Answering, we found that they had totally lost power, the engine stopped as well as the navigation equipment and they were working on it. "Standing by," was our answer as I throttled back the engine and tried to pick out our friends navigation lights against the backdrop of the island.

Soon a voice speaking Spanish came on the VHF and the best that I could understand, he was admonishing *Dreamy* for coming to close to the Navy Base. This kept up for several minutes and finally, *Dreamy* announced that their motor was running; however their electronics were still out and they were going to come towards us, then follow along until Roy could repair their navigation system.

Relived, I throttled up and started looking for our friends. No more than ten minutes passed and we received another frantic call from *Dreamy* telling us to back off, that we were about to run into their stern. I immediately cut the throttle and went up on deck to take a look.

Dreamy was nowhere in sight so Norma called them on the radio to let them know it wasn't us on their stern. They continued to insist we were, they could see our masthead light now high above them and I detected the fright in their voices.

Soon they announced that the boat astern had just disappeared and wanted to know our position. We exchanged lat and longs and determined they were a half-mile ahead of us and I went below and switched on our radar to verify. Just the two of us were out there and I was relieved to see the green dot representing *Dreamy* on the radar screen exactly where he said he was.

Soon, it was our turn to see a boat coming up quickly on our stern out of the blackness. She was much larger and faster than us and I decided to contact them on the VHF—no answer and nothing on radar or the AIS. I don't remember seeing her running lights, only an eerily yellow tinted masthead light, now high above our stern and coming fast. I check with *Dreamy* and became convinced that it wasn't them, throttled up and changed course radically to avoid collision.

Norma was watching intently off our stern and as I turned, she was able to make out the silhouette of an old square-rigger sailing ship just before it vanished in the darkness. It was nowhere to be found. We sat silently in the cockpit just thinking about the evening's events and decided it all probably didn't really happen—at least that's my story and I'm sticking to it!

Large ship traffic started appearing in a couple of hours and we took turns standing watch while the other slept. We were both awake the following morning to witness the unbelievably beautiful shoreline of Cancun passing by with its distinctly shaped hotels and even an old Mayan ruin setting high atop a cliff.

Happy Ours and *Dream Odyssey* both anchored in Isla Mujeres at about the same time and were greeted warmly by fellow cruisers as we participated in the eight AM radio net that had just been announced.

Choosing to hire an agent for check in, we headed for Marina Paraiso to find Hosey, the one recommended by our fellow cruisers.

The marina itself was a little bit of paradise with a swimming pool, nice docks and an open serve yourself honor bar that offered ice cold beer, water and soft drinks at a very reasonable price; however, the best was yet to come.

Often when traveling, we met marina owners that were both friendly and helpful but Tom Boyland and his beautiful wife set a new standard for kindness and helpfulness. No matter that we were not staying in their marina, they saw to it that all of our questions were answered and that we were made welcome.

The check in process in Mexico is a little confusing, even with an agent, but with Tom's help, we knew where to go and what we needed to do. Just when we thought the check in was complete, we learned that we needed to take the water taxi over to Cancun and pay additional fees to import our boats—a one-time process that was necessary if we wanted to move into a marina or stay in the country for thirty days or more (one version). This was to be the first of many water taxi rides to Cancun and we enjoyed letting some one else drive for a change while we took in the sites.

The anchorage had a reputation for poor holding during storms and we knew that the only way we would leave *Happy Ours* and do inland travel was to take her into a marina. We asked Tom about securing a slip in his already full marina and in a couple of days, we heard his cheerful voice on the VHF asking if we were ready to come in. He had moved some boats around so he could accommodate a boat our size with its six-foot draft and soon we were safely in a slip in Marina Paraiso and ready to explore the area.

We enjoyed the twenty-minute walk to town and fell in love with the touristy, laid back atmosphere. Beaches, bars, souvenir shops and restaurants were plentiful and taxis were available to take us back to the boat incase we ate, drank, or bought too much.

I immediately ordered our snail mail from Voyagers Mail Service and caught up on all our email using the marina's Internet. Our mail arrived with in a week but was held up by Customs because it contained our prescription medicine. We had never had this problem before and needed our prescriptions so we talked to Tom about our problem. He told us to take a copy of our prescription to a pharmacy in town and they would fill it even though it was not an original.

Truth is we really didn't need a prescription and it was no problem getting what we needed. We negotiated a good price and all that remained to do was to figure out how to get our mail. Hosey knew the Customs agent and after we agreed to pay the postage amount required to send the package back to the Voyagers Mail Service, we had Seth remove the medicine and re-ship our mail.

When it arrived, it contained an SSCA Bulletin with a story about Marina Pariso being a new cruising station. Having read it, I gave the publication to Tom who had not yet seen the article about him and the marina. He was really excited to see it and I jokingly mentioned that we should have a gam—a get together of SSCA members and those who would be interested in learning about the organization.

Just a few weeks had passed and Tom came by our boat and proudly announced he would be hosting a gam that weekend! When the initial shock ended, Norma and I quickly downloaded membership material and prepared to set up an information table. We asked fellow SSCA members Eric and Carol Wood from *Drift Wood* to help us set things up and man the table. I announced the event on the net each morning and coordinated details with Tom.

What a party! Tom had hired a ten-piece mariachi band to entertain and set up tables and chairs to provide a free BBQ meal to all 60 people in attendance. New Commodores were sponsored as well as some interested cruisers signed up for membership. We took pictures to document the event and thanked Tom and his wife for being such great hosts.

Norma promoted a Mexican Train domino game that was held in the little bar at the marina every Sunday and with Roy and Michel, we felt very much at home. This coupled with the SSCA activities allowed us to meet many new cruisers and the marina was filled to capacity with new friends. Tom seemed to look for things to entertain us and sponsored potlucks and cookouts nearly every week, maintaining a fantastic party like atmosphere.

We met a friendly fellow down town who ran a travel agency. He showed us that by attending a time share presentation in Cancun we would not only be treated to a fantastic buffet in a five star resort but also would be furnished free tickets to some of the expensive Mayan tours on the mainland.

Roy, Michel, Norma, and I along with Doug from *Erie* agreed to give it a try and it was certainly worth doing. We took the water taxi using furnished tickets and were picked up by a van that was waiting. He drove us to a very nice resort where we were introduced to a sales representative who led us to a first class buffet where we gorged ourselves with good things to eat.

An interesting tour of the resort followed, ending in a high-pressure sales presentation. We were then given our free tour tickets and then taken back to the ferry. All went well and we certainly recommended this to our fellow cruisers.

The following day we headed for Cancun and once again, a van was waiting to take us to a place where we boarded a much larger bus and headed for the Coba ruins.

These ruins were very much like the ones we visited in Honduras and Guatemala but not nearly as well preserved. Our tour guide was very knowledgeable and the day passed quickly as he told us about this ancient place and the people who lived here.

It was dark when we returned to Cancun and the bright city lights reminded us of those we had seen in Los Vegas. Tourists were everywhere and there was much to do. By the time we returned to Isla Mujeres, we took a taxi to the boats, being way too tired to do the twenty-minute walk.

"Tulum by the Sea," the ruins we had admired on the way in, was only a short hop from the water taxi terminal in Cancun and we couldn't wait to visit them. They looked out over the beautiful blue ocean, which was decorated by white foamy waves marking the underwater reefs, which for centuries have protected the city from unwanted intrusion. Our guide told us that there was a way to bring supply boats in safely thru the reef but only with help from the locals and this had been a major trading center for the Mayans.

It was thought that Tulum was a birthing center for upper-class women and the architecture had been made especially beautiful. Even the remains, after all these centuries, have a sort of charm missing in the other Mayan ruins that we visited.

Another fascinating attraction is Chichen Itza, a Mayan ruin named by its close proximity to the mouth of a well. It is a three-hour drive from the water taxi terminal in Cancun and we used the services of a tour company, which provided us an English-speaking guide. This site has been voted one of the new Seven Wonders of the World and for us; it lived up to its new status.

Most impressive to me was the Pyramid of Kukulcan. It represents the Mayan Calander and is constructed of 91 steps leading to the top on each side with the final platform at the top. This figures to be 91x4=364+1(the top platform) = 365 days in the year. Each side has 52 panels representing a 52-year cosmic cycle, which marks the end of the old and the beginning of the new in their culture. There is much more to it than this and there are scholars who have dedicated their lives to the study of such things and have published books and articles on this fascinating subject. I have noticed that there is often disagreement among them.

A couple of interesting features: At the equinoxes, a triangular shaped shadow slowly slithers up or down the side of the pyramid to join or leave a carved snake head indicating the time to plant and the time to harvest.

Most amazing to us was that when you clap your hands loudly in front of the pyramid, a loud squawking sound emanates from the top as if the ancient serpent is still answering. We were told it used to respond to the drums during a ceremony and one can only guess for what purpose.

Other attractions included the largest ball court than we'd seen anywhere. It differed from others in that it had very high vertical walls and extra high goals. I'm not sure but it is believed that the captain of the loosing (some say the winning) team was beheaded and his heart was removed and placed on the stone Chac-Mool statue as a blood sacrifice during a wild post-game ceremony. There is even a nearby carving of a plumed warrior holding an ax with a severed head laying on the ground beneath it and the symbol in his other hand representing a human heart.

There were many things in this vast complex that we missed seeing or understanding because the sun was hot and our guide was fat and lazy. Rather than staying with us, he would find some shade and talk to death what ever could be seen from that vantage point. He then sent us on our own without a map to explore what remained and we vowed to return later, having picked up some literature written in Spanish about a light show that was available in the evenings.

On the way back to the boat, the bus stopped briefly at a Cenote. It is basically a sinkhole with water down below and there are many of these throughout Mexico. Mayans would often drop people in them as a sacrifice and divers have found the bottoms to be littered with bones and artifacts.

This particular one had stone steps carved in a tunnel leading to the water at the bottom. As we reached the bottom, the tunnel opened into a giant dark cavern. The water, illuminated by the sunlight flowing in from the tiny hole far above, glowed an emerald green in the center giving way to darker shades, then darkness as the effects of the sun faded away. Some people were swimming in the pool while the rest of us wore out our cameras trying to capture the eerie beauty of this magical place.

Dream Odyssey announced it was time for them to leave, and several of our new friends, seeing the weather window, went with them. Norma and I had no obligations to be anywhere before hurricane season and opted to stay and further explore this paradise. We spent the last evening with our friends, having dinner in town. Michel gave us this poem that she had written in honor of our traveling together and it is something we cherish:

> *It is About the Journey*
> *In a "Cruisers" life……*
> *There are those we meet along the way*
> *that touch us more than others.*
> *They may or may not be similar in age,*
> *education, occupation or any other*
> *"considered-normal" milestones…*
> *but that is part of the beauty of it.*
> *We move like gypsies……*

*Gypsies of the sea,
Mobicentric.... driven by seasons & weather,
demons or angels of the past.
Driven by destinations, goals,
dreams, schedules   Driven!
The eternal search for the next paradise.
But along the journey...
It is the people we encounter
who actually make the Odyssey ...
One worth taking! If it were not for them....
Our stories could not be told
Could not be shared
Could not be remembered!
On this journey.... You have become our Friends!
Other soul mates that feel the heart beat of the sea
& cherish the moments we have had
to share this awesome experience.
This life has given us many Treasures
during our sojourn upon the sea...
& one of those treasures has been
the Two of You!*

*For Bob & Norma Morris
S/V Happy 'Ours*

**Written by Michelle Parsons
S/V Dream Odyssey (& Roy too!)
March 2009**

We felt emptiness after they left but life goes on and new friends kept us occupied. Jack and Jo on *Mystic Adventure* pulled in to the harbor and it was really good to see them again. They had problems getting a slip in our marina but Tom insisted he could accommodate them.

He brought in dredging equipment and tried to make a slip deep enough; however, it took several dinks at high tide to drag them in across the sandy bottom. Tom continued to dredge around their keel and finally the *Mystic Adventure* was floating in her slip.

Jack and Jo were spoiling for a game of cards called "Oh Hell," and we caught up on old times as we played. We learned that Jack's daughter, Cindy was coming soon and I excitedly told Jack about the special light show at Chitin Itza and what a wonderful place it was. We soon were making plans for obtaining private transportation and found accommodations for an overnight stay near the ruins.

Soon the five of us were on our way for another adventure, it was different taking a private bus and being on our own but we had done this before in many different countries that were not nearly as tourist orientated as Cancun and survived. The bus dropped us off near our hotel and Jo opted to eat lunch with us while Jack and Cindy headed for a cave tour. When it was time to pay our bills at the restaurant, Joe discovered her little purse was missing from her backpack. We remembered her putting it under the seat on the bus and we all had napped on the way there. Some one in the seat behind her must have stolen her purse from the backpack and gotten off the bus while we were napping.

We checked in at the hotel after lunch and waited for Jack and Cindy to return. When he found out what had happened, Jack immediately called to stop his credit card only to find out purchases had already been charged to it in Spain! He was told that the card company had already placed a hold on his card and a new one would soon be issued to him.

We ate a quick supper at the hotel restaurant, and then took a taxi to Chitian Itza, arriving just in time for the light show. It was all in Spanish with strange music in the background and our eyes blinked as the great pyramid changed colors and the lights simulated the serpent descending down its side. From time to time the pyramid would go dark and the lights would illuminate the various temples surrounding the area and an explanation of their purpose was given.

I noticed we were about the only non-local spectators there and was pleased that we all had advanced enough to be comfortable and just enjoy the show.

The next morning, a hotel van dropped us off directly at the ruins and we quickly found a guide at the visitor center and negotiated a price for his services. We were amazed with his knowledge and professionalism and he literally wore us out as we went from ruin to ruin—much different than our previous experience had been.

We enjoyed a good night's sleep, then stood along the highway in front of the hotel, waiting for a bus to take us back to Cancun. One finally arrived and we all put our luggage in the overhead so we could keep an eye on it. Jo decided to return directly to the water taxi with us and left Jack and Cindy to tour Tulum without her. It was obvious that Jo was still in pain with her ankle and needed to rest.

After resting a couple of days we rented a golf cart and toured the island of Isla Mujeres with Jack and Cindy—Joe had workers on the boat and thought it best not to leave. We visited a lighthouse, turtle farm, dolphin encounter, a fine restaurant, and an interesting little park located on the southern tip of the island. It housed both a Mayan ruin and modern sculptures and was a fun place to visit. We watched as Cindy enjoyed a zip line ride out over the ocean and back, then the day was gone. I don't think we missed seeing anything on the island!

It was late April and time for *Happy Ours* to move on in order to get to St. Pete before hurricane season. We had reservations at St Pete Municipal Marina for mid May and still wanted to spend some time in the Dry Tortugas. Jim on *More Fun* had befriended us and suggested we call Mike, a friend of his to help us clear back in to the US. He researched it for us and found that during the week, we could report to the St Pete airport instead of going thru the hassle of appearing in Tampa.

Jack and Jo were still working on their boat and had no definite plan to travel so we checked out of Mexico and headed for the Dry Tortugas on our own.

Chapter 19

Back to the USA

We expected to get a little boost from the current, but there never seemed to be much help; however, *Happy Ours* enjoys a close reach and she made good time heading to windward. Probably the most difficult part of our journey was to pass by Cuba without stopping for a visit. Oh well, maybe we can fly down there when it becomes legal.

The wind and seas calmed down and we motored our way into the anchorage in front of Ft Jefferson. Several yachts were there but there was plenty of room. The anchorage is fairly exposed and we had chosen the perfect weather for being there. Staying clear of a big commercial mooring buoy, we dropped the hook nearly in front of the fort entrance, but quite a ways off from it, all the while drinking in the majesty of this monstrous brick structure in the middle of no where.

I quickly closed the thru-hull valves that allowed overboard discharge and for the first time in eight years, set things up to pump into our holding tank in compliance with the no dumping regulations. I noticed a y-valve was frozen and instructed Norma to use only the forward head until things were sorted out and joined her in the cockpit for a glass of celebratory wine. We spent that evening on board, tiding up both *Happy Ours* and ourselves and relived our beautiful sail from Mexico over a late, quiet supper.

The next morning found me working on the y-valve—try as I would, it would not budge. Finally, I removed the three stainless steal hose clamps and wrestled the valve from the clutches of its three respective hoses.

Placing a bucket underneath proved unnecessary, as the valve looked like some one had poured concrete in it and let it set up. Taking it and the bucket up into fresh air and sunlight, I started chiseling away at the obstruction with the help of a large screwdriver and a hammer. It had only taken an hour to knock most of the nasty stuff clear and I decided to finish cleaning it by soaking it in a product called CLR.

Pouring some of this wonderful stuff into my bucket and adding water, I dropped the valve in to soak. Shortly, I removed the valve and when I rinsed it off, it looked like new. By alternately exercising the valve handle and injecting silicone grease into the moving parts, the valve began to work smoothly and was soon ready to re-install.

Taking it down below, I sat cross-legged in the floor, squeezed my upper body and arms into the lavatory cabinet and started the installation. It was hot and smelly in there, causing me to work swiftly at the task at hand.

All of a sudden, there was a terrible rumbling in the pipes and then the unthinkable happened. Norma had used the forward head and as she was pumping away to empty the bowl, nasty, horrible chunks of the brown concrete blew out all over me, followed by the foulest smelling blackish liquid I'd ever encountered. The pipe hadn't leaked earlier because it had been obstructed with the same stuff that was in the valve and it had chosen this opportune time to clear its throat.

I was speechless—a good thing for I dared not open my mouth. Norma asking, "Honey, what's that smell" momentarily stopped in her tracks as she saw what had happened, then almost ran up the stairs into the cockpit, not knowing what may happen next.

I just climbed into the bathtub clothes and all and turned on the shower to wash off the nasty stuff, then began cleaning up the mess. That being done, I installed the valve, checked it for leaks, then re-showered with antibacterial soap and changed clothes. I wasn't hungry and knocked down a couple of rum n colas in honor of the occasion instead. Being in no mood to tour the fort that day, I just found a good book to read and laid back on a nice comfy pillow in the cockpit.

Norma headed below with Clorox water to add her special touch to the clean up effort but even that couldn't totally eliminate the odor. It took several days for things to get back to normal. She put my clothes in a shell-collecting bag and hung them over the side for a good saltwater soaking—over night seemed to do the trick.

Things started going well and we launched the dink for the first time since we had arrived and explored the anchorage. One of the islands had been marked off limits and was inhabited by several species of birds. Seeing it was not too exciting, as we had walked unencumbered among the nesting birds in several other countries.

A large tour boat had pulled up to the fort entrance and the place was crawling with tourists so we opted to return to *Happy Ours*, have lunch and just hang out. We were doing just that when several Island Packet sailboats came in and anchored. Devin and Liz Tailor from *Moose Tracks*, the friendliest of the bunch, immediately dinked over and introduced themselves.

We learned that the group had sailed down from the St Pete area and were on a holiday. Devin told us the two of them have plans to go cruising with in the next couple of years and were interested to hear some of our stories. They in turn, caught us up on the latest news in St Pete. We all hit it off and enjoyed each other's company, especially when Devin and I learned our birthdays were going to happen within the next couple of days and we decided to celebrate them together.

To make matters even better, Jack and Jo sailed in that evening and anchored in the overflow area. In a couple of days, Jo baked us a wonderful cake and hosted the birthday party on the *Mystic Adventure*.

Norma and I decided that *Moose Tracks* should have a Moose call, labeled a conk horn as such and presented it as a gift to Devin. We introduced them to the time honored tradition of blowing a conk horn each night at sunset and was surprised that Liz could make the thing sound as mellow as a trumpet.

We finally toured the fort and snorkeled in its clear surrounding waters. We learned that Fort Jefferson was constructed on a sand base with footing two feet thick, fourteen feet wide and a mile long. It was to be a three-tier fort, housing over 400 guns and was constructed of sixteen million bricks.

The pitiful thing about it was that it never was really completed and represents a colossal waste of taxpayers' money. It was used as a prison during the civil war and was home to Dr. Samuel A Mudd who was imprisoned there for treating the wounds of John Wilkes Booth. He distinguished himself by treating inmates and soldiers alike during an epidemic of yellow fever that nearly wiped out the fort's entire population. Another yellow fever out brake, followed by a devastating hurricane, led the Army to close the fort in 1874.

All too soon, it was time for us to up anchor and head for St. Pete. Jack and Jo were in a hurry and already left, motoring most of the way. Devin and Liz wanted to go to Ft Myers Beach to finish off their Holiday, so they headed out a little later than us. *Happy Ours* had only a half tank of fuel and Norma and I had a burning desire to sail across our track—the same one we had made eight years ago. We left at first light, hoisting sail (rolling it out) and heading north. We set our course straight for Tampa Bay and planned to take time out the next morning to hoist the flags of all the countries we had visited from the flag halyards and make a grand entrance—Not!

We encountered several storms during the night on the way up and daylight found us with all sails drawing and the motor running, trying to get in before the next front arrived. Flying the flags didn't happen and seemed unimportant as *Happy Ours* flew under the beautiful Skyway Bridge at full speed.

By 11:30 that morning, the dock master at St. Pete Municipal Marina was assisting us with our lines as we pulled into a slip on their new dock. It was Friday morning and there wasn't a moment to spare if we wanted to check in at the airport in St. Pete because customs closed there at five p.m.

We called Mike, as our friend Jim in Isla Mujeres had instructed, and he drove to the marina and picked us up. In no time we found the customs office and were officially back in the good old USA.

By the time Mike returned us to *Happy Ours*, the storm had caught up with us and it lasted off and on for the following three days, with strong winds and torrential rain. We were truly glad to be safely in the marina.

We contacted Penny O Flattery, a cruiser and real estate agent we had been in email contact with and asked her to show us some condos. Next, we flew to Kansas City to pick up our little red Pontiac and visit with friends and family.

Before we were ready to leave KC, Penny sent us an email with attached pictures displaying a condo in Gulfport with a beautiful water view and she insisted we return to take a look at this new offering.

We drove back to Florida that week, loved the place, made an offer and soon were proud owners. It took several weeks to paint and clean it up to Norma's standards and to find some furniture to make it home. Gulfport is a funky little town, with its own beach, plenty of restaurants and bars, entertainment, artist, authors, as well as over and underachievers. It provides us nearly the same atmosphere that we found so enjoyable in the Caribbean and we are happy to call this place home.

We cleaned *Happy Ours* up, unloaded our personal belongings and put her on the market, listing her with a fellow SSCA member, Harry at Edwards Yachts. Maintaining the option to sell her, I prepared a web site and made a few for sale listings of our own. It took several months in a poor economy for Harry to find a buyer and oddly enough, a couple from Columbia, Missouri purchased *Happy Ours*. It appears more Missourians will soon be loose in the Caribbean and *Happy Ours* will once again glide happily along in the warm waters as she enjoys new adventures.

Some neighbors and friends had invited us to spend New Years Eve at the Bocus Ciega Yacht Club and that is where this story began.

Chapter 20

Just for Cruisers and the Curious

I have done my best to write something that is both informative and entertaining for most audiences; however there are certain topics that Norma and I want to share with those who may be just starting out and would like to hear our opinion.

An in-depth discussion perhaps will be covered in a future volume but for now this should suffice in introducing the reader to some general cruising information.

The Cruising Budget is a topic we wrestled with for a long time. It is illusive information—where some one cruises and the type of boat, equipment and the amount of inland travel that they choose will determine cost. Staying in marinas proved very expensive but was necessary for leaving the boat for any length of time. We felt comfortable leaving *Happy Ours* anchored overnight by herself on very few occasions and then only under the watchful eye of a trusted fellow cruiser. Here is Norma's budget for a year to give the reader an idea of some of our expenses—it is already obsolete as prices change rapidly:

Boat Expense		Food/drink	Enertainmemt/Car	Marina	Eating out/bar	Misc		Total
misc boat		33	81.78 Taxi	85 slip	357	160 Health Ins	374	
Gen parts	463.71	124.31 Water taxi	41 Electric	117	69 Yahoo	5	
Gen parts		730.39	5 Printer Ink	22 curising permit	79	40 Hair cut	12	
			353.74 Emergration	20 Laundry	5	273 Misc	58	
			200.29 Computer speakers	13 Propane	13	37 Medical/drugs	273	
			Buss	28 Boat watching	10	News paper	2	
			Hotel	87 Tax	20	Gambling	5	
			Xmas gifts	150		Doctor	20	
						Canvas	148	
						Tools	81	
						Phone card	12	
Jan 2008 totals		1227.	765.12	446	601	579		990 4608
Gas tank		44	187 Taxi	8 slip	246	235 Health Ins	374	
OB tune up		35	150 Water taxi	36 Electric	121	184 Yahoo	5	
Boat parts		38	Emergration	20 Laundry	23	Mail	39	
			DVD player	40 Tax	13	Medical/drugs	35	
			Shipping	5		Misc	2	
						Phone card	13	
Feb 2008 totals		117	337	109	403	419		468 1853
Refrigerator repair		205	285 Customs	54 slip	399	113 Health ins	374	
Bottom cleaning		42	87 port captain	9 electric	166	52 Yahoo	5	
Wash/wax		55	37 water taxi tours	6 laundry	30	97 Misc	23	
Sea tow bill		149	van rental	12 tax	21	hair cut	20	
Duct tape		6		34 trash	2	medical/drugs	5	
Fuel/Diecel		341	Emergration tips	100 dock fees"	10	internet	3	
Fuel/gas		48		2		tool	78	
misc		27						
March 2008 totals		873	409	217	628	262		508 2897

Boat Expense	Food/Drink	Enertinment/car/travel		Marina		Eating out/bar	Misc		Total
		122	Customs	6	laundry	8	52	yahoo	5
		45	taxi	78	slip	216	97	Misc	36
		115	tips	8	dinkdock	5	114	cook book	29
		140	airline tickets	1589				purchased phone	43
			car insurance	151				xmas decoration	8
			sirius radio	120				phone cards	15
			credit cardfee	125				movies	6
			tours	15				haircut	33
								dentist	60
								doctor	63
								medical/drugs	201
								Health ins	374
Aprl 08 total		422		2092		229	263		873 3879
Dink fuel	80	49	car mtc	67	slip	302	82	health ins	374
dink ob repair	55	31	book	32	electricity	25	131	misc	109
Boat parts	179	30	electronics'	16	laundry	30	306	yahoo	5
yact equipt'	809	43	ear plugs	14	propane	11	298	med/drugs	102
Forespar	72		new dive card	16	water	3		clothes	194
Balmar regulators	359		office max	45	slip	247		bank card	13
watermaker parts	148		buss ticket	38	misc	86		phone chip	7
sirius antenna	90		tour	114				clothes	295
misc	92		hotel	100				walmart	116
			taxi	37				voyager mail serv	199
			customs/entergation	283				mail	27
			water taxi'	30					
			usps dues	90					
			car fuel	75					
			car wash	6					
			gifts	600					
			misc	66					
May 08 Total	1884	153		1629		704	817		1441 6628

Boatnuts Loose in the Caribbean

Boat Expense		Food/drink	Enertainment/car/travel		Marina		Eating out/bar	Misc		Total	
Flag	29	88	usps meeting	96	slip	247		98	health ins	374	
misc	65	116	car fuel	221				144	yahoo	5	
		92	computer stuff	32				75	medical/drugs	32	
		13	gift	27				80	power ball	9	
			camera exp	54					misc	138	
			donation	10					clothes	126	
			hotel	146					clothes	47	
			branson show	60					reading glasses	10	
			tax school	104					camcorder	450	
			diver dan dues	79					luggage	36	
			misc	6					mail	6	
June 08 totals	94	309		835		247		397		1233	3115
stantion boards	75	135	Car fuel	199	Slip	247		113	health ins	374	
garmin charts	240	35	boat us dues	13	laundry	8		103	yahoo	5	
		45	storage tubs	39				222	phone	9	
			car wash	15				139	books	13	
			gifts	40					clothes	31	
			hotel	144					power ball	5	
			hotel	73					med/drugs	127	
			luggage	19					phone chips	21	
			stamps	9					credit card fee	95	
			car oil change	22					misc	78	
			phone calls	5							
			mail	20							
			phone cards	43							
			car storage	550							
			water taxi	7							
			bus	22							
			taxi	8							
			spanish class book	36							
			misc	20							
July 08 totals	315	215		0	1284	0	255	577		0	758 3404

Boat Expense		Food/drink	Entertainment/car/travel		Marina		Eating out/bar		misc		Total
varnish	157		345	Water taxi	30	slip	247		93	Health ins	374
engine belt	3		88	buss tickets	18	laundry	30		281	yahoo	5
dink motor part	31		135	Water taxi	6	Elect.	148		53	med/drugs	46
				tour	76					phone card	7
				map	3					hair cut	7
				tips	4					ear rings	17
										misc	11
Aug 08 totals	191		568		137		425		427		467 2215
varnish labor	335		14	misc	15	slip	255		84	Health ins	374
dink cover	100		127	buss tickets	35	laundry	188		336	misc	2
boat insurance	392		69	hotel	135	electricity	18		97	hair cut	7
survey	435			water taxi	8					phone card	7
canvas work	120			bug spray	6					med/drugs	95
generator part	17			donation	14					yahoo	5
Sept 08 totals	493		210		213		461		517		490 6823
dink fuel	25		158	buss ticket	72	slip	306		166	Health ins	374
boat registration	203		26	taxis	101	laundry	38		236	misc	10
cable ties	15		207	tours	100	electricity	194		623	med/drug	291
			54	hotel	487				77	mail	64
				tips	9					haircuts	11
				water taxi	25					phone card	7
				misc	175					movies	14
										canvas	60
										gifts	18
										clothes	10
										jewelry	40
										yahoo	7
										doctor	598
Oct 08 totals	243		445		969		538		1102		1504 4801

Boatnuts Loose in the Caribbean

Boat Expense		Food/drink	Enertainment/car/travel		Marina		Eating out/bar	misc		Total
Starter batteries	301		101 car ins		186 slip	306		126 Health ins	374	
canvas work	500		178 tour		49 electricity	138		101 phone cards	27	
boat registration	202		245 ink cartridge		15 laundry	25		109 medical/drug	178	
dink fuel	14		21 google earth		20			mail	26	
davit work	103		gifts		27			yahoo	7	
boat wax	42							Sail Mail dues	250	
Buffer	70							prescriptiona	81	
graphics painting	60							misc	5	
Nov 08 totals	1292		545		297		469	336		948	3887
Davit braces	358		186 water taxi		14					
Fuel, diecel	186		246 gifts		336 slip	306		152 Health ins	374	
fuel, dink	53		27 car license		102 electricity	143		24 yahoo	7	
varnish materials	54		137		laundry	24		147 med/drugs	28	
fuel treatment	35		1216		propane	15		92 mail	52	
			11					phone cards	27	
								doctors	98	
								movies	7	
								misc	20	
Dec 04 totals	686		1823		452		488	415		613	4477

Eating out expense lists only a few entries—we ran a tab in the marina restaurant and this includes parties, food and drink. We were in a marina most of the time in the Rio Dulce and did a lot of inland travel as well as a trip home that year. There was an unusual medical expense because of a superficial staff infection I came down with.

We used Voyagers Mail Service in Islamorada, Florida to take care of our mail. For a small fee, they provided us a mailing address and would collect our mail and even sort out the junk if we wanted them to. When we sailed into a place that we planned to stay a while, I could either call or send an email to have our mail sent to us. They would determine which was the most efficient method to send it, box it up, mark it Yacht in Transit, and we would have it in a week or two.

For communications, we started out using and Iridium Satellite phone but stopped using it as the cost kept elevating each year. Had we headed for the South Pacific however, it would have been an excellent thing to have. If Internet was available, we used Skype on the computer to call home. Some Internet cafes in town offered this service as well.

I replaced the old SSB radio with a new one and included a pactor modem that would let us use radio email. Licensed Ham Operators can use this service for free but forbids it being used for business. Sail Mail offers the service for a yearly fee and allows business communications—no extra license required other than the ships station license. The modem let us download weather fax and forecast directly into our laptop, which proved indispensable.

Nearly every country we planned to stay in for a while offered a pay as you go telephone at very reasonable prices. Although not really necessary, it was a nice convenience. We also carried a phone card from the States for international calls.

We found medical and dental services to be available nearly everywhere we went and the prices were surprisingly reasonable. I maintained a health insurance policy for the two of us the whole time we cruised and paid up to $ 700 a month to keep it. We rarely met the deductible, paying out of the country prices; however when Norma needed knee replacements, we went to the States for that procedure and were glad to have insurance.

A trip to the dentist was made every six months in whatever country we happened to be in for cleaning and the prices were very reasonable. We didn't have dental insurance and really didn't need it.

Fellow cruisers always knew of some one to recommend and most places had a morning radio net for the exchange of this information.

As far as provisions go, we started out with *Happy Ours* loaded with can goods thinking they would be difficult to find along the way. Nothing could be farther from the truth—nearly everywhere we went in the Caribbean, we easily replenished our supplies. Norma started buying fresh fruits and vegetables from the local markets and we learned to enjoy some different things. We caught fish along the way and were able to buy or barter lobster, crab and fish very reasonably.

Chicken was available nearly everywhere and was fresh and good—so fresh that it was still alive when we picked it out in one of the open markets! Beef in Venezuela was as good as any we have tasted and the butchers would cut it just the way you wanted it.

Boat parts were at a premium, if available at all, and a good supply of spares as well as the tools to install them proved to be a must. A maintenance manual on each piece of equipment was helpful as well as sometimes necessary. You are often on your own to fix things.

What to carry for spares is a topic of discussion among cruisers and there is never a consensus. For going off shore cruising, my bare minimum list would include:

A spare GPS
Spare light bulbs for everything
Water pump impellers for engine and generator
Fan belts for each
Spare zincs
A box of O-rings

An assortment of stainless steel washers, nuts, bolts, and screws
An assortment of stainless hose clamps
An assortment of stainless cotter pins
Spare butane torches for lighting the grill and stove
An assortment of crimp on electrical fittings
Heat shrink, electrical tape, rigging tape, duct tape and Teflon tape
Spare regulator and alternator or at least a rebuild kit for the alternator
Spare electric fuel pump
Spare portable battery charger
At least one back up for every water pump on board: a/c, fresh
Rebuild kits for each head (several)
Spare filters for everything and some oil
Some spare water hose, fittings and splices water, bilge, sump
Hose repair/splice kit for the engine
A set of round wooden tapered plugs
Spark plugs and fuel filter for the outboard
Sail repair tape, sail cloth
Refrigerant, tools and gauges necessary to service the refrigerator (depending on the type)
An assortment of bungee cords and Velcro straps
Heavy duty sewing machine that will do zig-zag stitch and thread
Various caulk and sealers
All purpose glue
Underwater type marine putty
A selection of various kinds of wire
A selection of various sizes of rope
A few spare turnbuckles, stay locks (for rigging) and blocks
An assortment of plastic cable ties
Packing for stuffing box (if you have that type)
A heavy board to use as a work bench and some clamps

The subject of refrigeration is a difficult one for me to discuss. The Grunert cold plate system on *Happy Ours* was never very reliable and used too much energy—even with space age insulation in the boxes. Other cruisers swore by the same system and never had a bit of trouble. I found the air-cooled system that I was able to install myself to be much more efficient and now there are keel cooled and other major changes available that I'm not familiar with.

Happy Ours had two 8D, 225 amp gel house batteries and two cranking batteries, one for the generator and the other for the engine. A Kiss high out put wind generator supplemented by three solar panels cut down on running the diesel generator and helped conserve fuel. A high output alternator coupled with a Balmar regulator and a Balmar duo charge device for isolating and charging the starting bank proved to be a worthwhile upgrade and served to backup the diesel generator if needed.

A large inverter/charger not only keeps the batteries topped off when plugged into shore power or when running the generator but allows the running of AC appliances such as the microwave directly from the house bank when under weigh.

Typically when arriving in a foreign country by boat, you anchor, hoist the yellow Q flag on the starboard spreader, dink in and find customs and immigration offices. A good cruising guide will tell the location and often provide a street map. Sometimes only the Captain with the crew's passports and paperwork is allowed to go in the first time and other countries may require everyone to appear. Bring your own ball point pen and of course plenty of money. You may need a credit or debit card to convert to local currency.

Above all, prepare to be polite and patient! The process can take a half-day or more and the immigration and customs offices may not be in the same place. Language is often a problem—not all the officials speak English.

Some officials are not very pleasant and seem to make things as difficult as possible. In Mexico, several officials wanted a tip in addition to the regular fees, even if we used an agent. A few countries such as Guatemala insisted on us hiring an agent to do the paperwork for an additional fee and directed us to an ATM to get local currency to pay with.

Other officials came out to our boat as soon as the anchor was down to inspect it and do the paperwork on the spot. Have fenders handy just incase.

No matter the procedure, it was always with a sigh of relief that I lowered the Q flag and hoisted the country's courtesy flag in its place. I tried to obtain the proper flags in advance, in some countries they were difficult to come by.

Checking out mirrored the check in and we learned to make sure to do neither of these on a weekend or one of their holidays as fees might quadruple. Usually we were given seventy-two hours to leave after checking out but Mexico insisted we leave immediately.

Here is a sample of the paperwork required for check in; I used this country because the forms were in English:

194   Boatnuts Loose in the Caribbean

NEDERLANDSE ANTILLEN
EILAND: _Curacao_

Datum ___ / ___ / 200__

TO BE USED I.C.W. THE CLEARING OF SCHIPS & YACHTS

Name of the ship	: Happy Ours
Type of ship	: FISH / FREIGHTER / TANKER / **SAILING VESSEL** / TUG / YACHT
Date of arrival / ~~departure~~	: 16 May 2005
Time of arrival / ~~departure~~	: 5pm
Last port of call	: Bonaire
Date dept. last port of call	: 15 May 2005
Next port of call	: Cartahegena
Date arrival next port of call	: 17 Aug 2005
Gross tonnage	: 26
Dead weight tonnage	: 23
Netto tonnage	: 23
Length in meters	: ~~16~~ 9 16
Beam in meters	: ~~39~~ ~~14~~
Draft in meters	: 2.8
Nationality / flag	: USA
Homeport	: Lee's Summit mo
Radio call sign	: WDA 3668
Name owner	: Norma Morris
Address owner	: ~~~~~~~~~~~~~~~~~ Islamorada FL
Name operator	: Robert & Norma Morris
Address operator	: same
Name agent	: None
Address agent	: None
Type motor	: Yanmar
Total H.P.	: 62
Registration number	: ~~~~~~~
Date registration	: Nov 2004
Place of registration	: USCG - ucb
Hull colour	: Tan
Particulars	:
Berth	: Spanish waters - Kima Keliki Marina
Name of Captain	: Robert & Norma Morris
Address of Captain	: same

I hereby declare the above particulars to be true

Signature Captain

SEE OTHER SIDE FOR CREWLIST / PASSENGERLIST

Nr	LAST NAME	FIRST NAME	BIRTH DATE	BIRTH PLACE	NATIONALITY	PASSPORT Nr	RANK / PASS	REMARKS
1	Morris	Robert		Missouri	USA		co-capt	
2	Morris	Diane		Missouri	USA		co-capt	

NETHERLANDS ANTILLES CUSTOMS CLEARANCE FORM

INBOUND 0	OUTBOND 0	ROTATION REF NO.:

VESSEL NAME: Happy Ours
OWNER: Norm Morris
REGISTRATION NO.: [illegible]
ADDRESS: Islamorada FL 33036

DATE OF ARRIVAL: 16/05/[year] DD MM YY   TIME OF ARRIVAL: 5pm HRS.   INTENDED DEPARTURE DATE: [illegible] DD MM YY
PORT OF ARRIVAL: Curacao   PURPOSE OF VISIT: Tourist
PREVIOUS PORT: Bonaire   PREVIOUS COUNTRY: Bonaire
NEXT PORT: Cartagena   NEXT COUNTRY: Colombia
CONTACT CELL/PHONE: none   GPS NO.: 2
TYPE OF VESSEL: Island Packet   NO. OF MASTS: 1   YEAR BUILT: 1992
CONSTRUCTION MATERIAL: Fiberglass   GROSS TONNAGE: 2[?]   COLOUR: Tan
HOME PORT: Key's Seafood M/V   COUNTRY OF REG: USA
VESSEL'S TOTAL LENGTH: 44   FEET/METRES   WIDTH: 13   FEET/METRES
OUTBOARD MOTOR: QUANTITY: BRAND: HP:
INBOARD MOTOR: QUANTITY: 1   BRAND: Yanmar   HP: [illegible]

CREW & PASSENGER LIST

FAMILY NAME	FIRST NAME	MASTER(M) CREW(C) PASS.(P)	NATIONALITY/ PLACE OF BIRTH	PASSPORT NO.	PLACE OF BIRTH DD/MM/YY
Morris	Robert	C	USA	[redacted]	[redacted]
Morris	Norm	C	USA	[redacted]	[redacted]

DO YOU HAVE WEAPONS ON BOARD? YES ☐   NO ☒   IF YES, PROVIDE DETAILS AS FOLLOWS:

Type(eg Pistol, Rifle)	Manufacturer	Serial No.	Calibre	Qty/Ammunition

I hereby declare that all information and particulars supplied on this form are true and correct.

Signed: [signature] (MASTER)   Date: 25/08/05   DD MM YY

COMMENTS:
DATE: 25 AUG 2005   OFFICER PROCESSING:

ON LEAVING, SURRENDER THE DUPLICATE FORM.
YOU HAVE BEEN ADMITTED WITH YOUR VESSEL TO THE NETHERLANDS ANTILLES FOR THE PERIOD STIPULATED HEREWITH
A FURTHER STAY, WITHOUT OBTAINING THE NECESSARY PERMIT FROM THE CUSTOMS OFFICE, IS ILLEGAL.
VALID: SIX (6) MONTHS AFTER DATE OF ISSUE.

AL SALIR ENTREQUE EL DUPLICADO.
USTED HA SIDO ADMITIDO EN LAS ANTILLAS NERLANDESAS CON SU LANCHA POR EL PERIODO QUE SE ESPICEFICA
EL PRESENTE.
EL PERMANECER DESPUES DE SU EXPIRACION SIN OBTENER DE LAS AUTORIDADES DE ADUANA UNA PROLOGA DEL MISMO,
CONSTITUYE UNA INFRACCION A LA LEY.
VALIDES: SEIS (6) MESES DE VIGENCIA DESPUES DE SU EXPEDICION.

Caribbean Customs Clearance Form
Netherlands Antilles

(✓) TICK THE APPROPRIATE BOX
INBOUND ☑   OUTBOUND ☐   ROTATION REF. NO.: ....

VESSEL NAME: Happy Ours   REGISTRATION #: 1105339
OWNER: Norma Morris   ADDRESS: ~~~~~~~~~~~
                                        Islamorada FL

DATE OF ARRIVAL: 15 / 5 / 2005   TIME OF ARRIVAL: 9⁰⁰ HRS.   INTENDED DEPARTURE DATE: 16 / 5 / 2005
PORT OF ARRIVAL: Williamstead   PURPOSE OF VISIT: Tourist
PREVIOUS PORT: Bonaire   PREVIOUS COUNTRY: Venezuela
NEXT PORT: Aruba / USA   NEXT COUNTRY: Aruba
CONTACT CELLPHONE: None   GPS No: 2 Garmin

TYPE OF VESSEL: Sail   NO. OF MASTS: 1   YEAR BUILT: 1992
CONSTRUCTION MATERIAL: Fiberglass   GROSS TONNAGE: 26   COLOUR: Tan
HOME PORT: Kris Sunset Mc   COUNTRY OF REG.: USA
VESSEL'S TOTAL LENGTH: 42 FEET/METRES   WIDTH: 13.1 FEET/METRES
OUTBOARD MOTOR: QUANTITY: ....   BRAND: Yamaha   HP: ....
INBOARD MOTOR: QUANTITY: 1   BRAND: Yanmar   HP: 62

CREW & PASSENGER LIST

	Family Name	First Name	Master/Crew/Passenger	Nationality/ Place of Birth	Passport #	Date of Birth DD/MM/YYYY
1.	Morris	Robert	M	USA	~~~~	~~~~
2.	Morris	Norma	C	USA	~~~~	~~~~
3.						
4.						
5.						
6.						

DO YOU HAVE WEAPONS ON BOARD?   YES ☐   NO ☑   IF YES, PROVIDE DETAILS AS FOLLOWS:
Type (eg Pistol, Rifle)   Manufacturer   Serial No.   Calibre & Qty Ammunition
None

I hereby declare that all information and particulars supplied on this form are true and correct.

Signed: ~~~~~~~~ (MASTER)   Date: 16 / 05 / 2005

COMMENTS:
DATE: 16 MEI 2005   OFFICER PROCESSING: ....

Many copies of the crew list as well as our documentation papers were required and a scanner and printer on board proved very helpful.

Electronic navigation using a GPS and electronic charts made life easy and we all exchanged waypoints with other cruisers; however, it was strictly up to us to check for accuracy.

I always kept a set of paper charts on hand for each destination—they didn't need to be the expensive color charts, Bluewater would sell us copies at a fraction of the cost.

Especially in the western Caribbean, cruising guides provided sketch charts of many out of the way anchorages available nowhere else and were worth their weight in gold.

I took Spanish classes when ever available and enjoyed being able to converse with the locals. It seemed to provide a bond not otherwise obtainable.

Norma and I could go on and on with these little tidbits but that seems beyond the scope of this book. We would have really liked to have seen some of this information before we went cruising and hope you find it useful.

****